Are You Stuck?
Is Life Passing You By?

Riley Harrison

The Blue Zebra Press

Are You Stuck?
Is Life Passing You By?

by Riley Harrison

Published by:
The Blue Zebra Press
Post Office Box 48597
Minneapolis, MN 55448 U.S.A.

Printed in the United States of America

CIP Data Availible

To Kathy, the love of my life, who showed me what's possible in life and to Edwin whose insights, support and editing made this book possible.

CONTENTS

Risk Taking   1
Accepting And Learning To Love
    Your Total Self   5
Identifying, Understanding And
    Managing Moods   11
Focus   15
The Ultimate Freedom – Choice   19
Questions   31
Does What You Believe Help You
    Or Harm You?   39
Affirmations   42
Surprise   47
Modeling   49
Changing Emotional States   55
Who Are You?   62
Taking Responsibility For One's Action   64
Don't Tell Me You Aren't Highly Creative   68
Demystifying Creativity   71
Capturing Creativity And Keeping It!   75
You Are Smarter Than You Think   79
Is That Cup Half Full Or Half Empty?   83
Positive Thinking   86
Moments To Remember   88
Cultivating Awareness   91
Fear   115
Thinking Big   129
Vagueness And Generalities: Enemies
    Of Personal Growth   132

CONTENTS

Beware Of Negative Influences   141
What's Wrong With Always Being Right?   145
Christmas Is It The Joy Of Giving
    Or The Depression Of Giving?   149
Money: Do You Control It
    Or Does It Control You?   151
Don't Worry, Be Happy   158
Why Use The Personals?   161
Blame   165
How Do We Get That Way
    And Why Do We Have These Problems?   167
Remembering The Past   171
The Portable Therapist   174
Tips From A Pro: How A Librarian Finds
    Good Books And More Time To Read   177
Inspiration   179
Do What You Love   180
Detachment   182
New Careers: Stressful Or Exciting?   184
The Second Time Around   190
Procrastination   195
Hidden Beliefs   198
On Fear Of Failure   202
Duty Or Delight?   204
Pampering The Senses   207
What Can I Do Differently?   210
Relationships   213
Contribution And Service   216
Letting Go   219

Introduction

Who am I and why am I writing another "self-help" book? I have always had a fascination with human potential. After many years of study, teaching self-empowerment seminars, writing articles, publishing a quarterly newsletter and providing counseling for those who are serious about changing their lives, I want to share what I've learned. I want to make you aware of your vast, untapped potential and the many exciting choices that are available to you.

Experts estimate that the average person only realizes about 5% of his potential. The mantras that I teach, chant and preach in all my classes are "Everyone has unrealized potential" and "we are all capable of leading much happier and much more fulfilling lives." I want you to understand the *real* reasons you feel stuck and provide you some tools, understanding and support to begin to really enjoy life. As Auntie Mame said, "Life is a banquet and most poor fools are starving to death".

We have been conditioned to believe that the route to happiness and contentment is the accumulation of money, wealth and material things. If that were the case, then all wealthy people would be happy and all kids would be depressed. That doesn't seem to be the case. I counsel many people who are extremely wealthy and also extremely depressed. My experience has been that the best route to happiness, fulfillment and serenity is through personal growth. The people that I encounter who are the happiest are those that are constantly growing and realizing their potential. Your potential should not be limited by some arbitrary, narrow definition of success (e.g. achieving financial goals, driving a BMW and living in the "right" neighborhood). It's much, much more. It means having work that you love, taking care of yourself emotionally and physically and having wonderful relationships in which you can give and receive love. It means having a purposeful existence and a reason to get up every morning.

This book is a collection of highly personal and hopefully insightful essays and observations that will enable me to share with you what I have learned. Some are short and some are long. There is no formulaic approach used in writing this book. I try to say what I feel needs to be said; no more or no less. This isn't a how-to-book, although it contains many specific strategies and techniques to improve your life. This is a book that addresses the real issues in life: your perception of yourself and how to change it in a positive way, your awareness of reality and learning to understand what is really happening and grasping the real reasons you are stuck in a life or existence that isn't working for you.

You are bombarded daily with opportunities to improve your life. However, if you lack the awareness to recognize opportunities or don't possess the courage to pursue them, you will remain stuck. If you are devoid of self confidence, blocked by fear, suffer from excessive worry or lack good risk taking skills life will be perceived as a somewhat hopeless and cruel struggle. As Pogo said " We have met the enemy and he is us".

When you begin to identify, acknowledge and deal with the real issues, life becomes grander and a joy to live. A good analogy is going from watching a show on an old black and white 12" TV set to viewing the same show on a 24" colored TV. You will never again be satisfied with your old TV set. A commitment to personal growth will change your life and give you insights that won't allow you to be comfortable with being stuck and living a stale, stagnant life.

I wish you the best. I am rooting for you and want to help you realize your potential in every facet of your existence.

Riley

Risk Taking

Some things do make you bigger, and taking risks is one of them. Not taking risks is the way we insist on staying small.

Julia Cameron

The reason many offer for being stuck and not living life on their terms is that they are not risk takers. But the biggest risk you run in life is settling and playing it safe. Does the risk-free life work? Ask yourself these two questions:

Do you wake up (always, often, never) looking forward to the day and anticipating with excitement all that the day holds in store for you?

Do you go to bed at night with a feeling of profound gratitude for experiencing an incredible and exciting day (always, often, never)?

If you haven't learned to be a risk taker, you will never be comfortable with your answers to those two questions. To risk may cause temporary anxiety, but not to risk will cause one to lose one's self.

The comfort zone is the real enemy to actualizing human potential. Our habits create well-worn ruts that become the path we travel. Instead of altering the path, we use our energies to make the path more comfortable and forget that if the path isn't going in the right direction, we have consigned ourselves to acceptance of the status quo, a life of underachievement and mediocrity.

It's not necessary to take large foolish risks (e.g., bet your paycheck on a horse race or obtain a second mortgage on your house to buy highly speculative stock). I'm not talking about behavior which requires confronting danger to prove that you are fearless or macho. I'm am talking about behavior that creates new feelings.

Change and new experiences initially cause unsettling feelings. We have a bias towards the status quo because that's what we know and are comfortable with. If we don't overcome the inertia of comfortable routines, we begin to experience a sameness and everyday begins to look and feel like the day before. We have to force ourselves to take risks, do new things and break these patterns that confine and prevent us from leading a more enjoyable, exciting and fulfilling life.

You can ask yourself a series of questions to help you identify the action that needs to be taken and to better understand and assess the degree of risk involved:

What is one risk you are currently considering?

Why is it important for you to take the risk?

If you took the risk and failed, what is the worst possible outcome?

If this approach fails, what are your other options? How could you deal with the outcome, if it is unsatisfactory?

Start with small risks, experiences that take you just outside of your comfort zone. Risk taking is an acquired skill and as you begin to take small risks, you will gain confidence and will trust yourself to undertake larger risks. Fear distorts our perspective and we have trouble evaluating how risky something might be. Taking small risks provides you experiences that allow you to be more objective as to what is at stake and you learn that many ventures aren't as risky as you imagine. To practice risk taking diminishes fear. You can become a better risk taker by committing to taking a small risk daily for a month. Everyday take a small step over that demarcation line into that scary unknown territory that lurks just outside your comfort zone. Every time you venture out of your comfort zone, your comfort zone is permanently expanded and can never shrink back to its original size.

I always tell myself that if a contemplated action makes me feel uncomfortable, it is probably something I need to do (make those phone calls, introduce myself to that stranger, tell a friend that what he or she is doing irritates the hell out of me, say no to that person who is intimidating or whose feelings will be hurt).

If you are a shy person, you may need to commit to starting a conversation with a stranger every day for a month. Next time you are waiting in line to buy a ticket for a movie, turn around and talk to the person behind you, regardless of age, sex or attractiveness. Make small talk with the person waiting at the bus stop or sitting next to you on the bus. If they don't respond, that's OK; they might also be shy. The next time you see that person, just smile and say, "Hi" or "How is it going?"

If you are not assertive and have compulsive people-pleasing tendencies and you find yourself constantly saying "Oh, that's OK," when really it isn't or "It really doesn't matter," when really it does, begin being more assertive in small ways. Start out with tiny steps. Next time you are having breakfast and the eggs are runny, or the hamburger at lunch is undercooked, ask the waitress to take it back and prepare it properly.

If you lack confidence, next time you go to a seminar, sit in the front rather than in the back. If you have ever left a seminar wishing you had participated more or asked a certain question, commit to asking three questions at the next seminar you attend.

When overcoming fear by developing better risk-taking skills, start small and go at your own pace. You want to learn how to push through you natural resistance to change. You don't want the risk to be so big or overwhelming that it creates immediate paralysis and shame.

As you develop your risk-taking skills, you will experience less anxiety during periods of sudden change. It will be easier for you to "go with the flow" and to accept the ebbs and flow of life.

Accepting And Learning To Love Your Total Self

**The curious paradox is that
when I accept myself just as I am,
then I can change.**

Carl Rogers

Seeing and learning to accept the totality of ourselves (both the good and the bad) is the first step on the road to greater compassion for other people and ourselves. We all have our dark side and share shameful impulses and thoughts (lust, greed, anger, impatience, etc.). These are part of our total identity. We have to learn how to accept and live with these desires and thoughts in order to become healthy and whole. When we deny or disown aspects of ourselves, we expend tremendous amounts of energy trying to suppress and keep submerged these baser instincts. Rather than learning acceptance, which leads to serenity, peace and a higher level of energy, we begin to develop a facade and false fronts that we present to others. When we deny our authentic selves, we cease being real and become poseurs. Phoniness breeds contempt and distrust, whereas authenticity provides for the possibility of real connection and intimacy. We begin to play the games listed below and live false roles that mask our true identity:

I am always charming, engaging, entertaining and amusing. Count on me to be the life of the party.

I am so sweet and nice. Can't you tell? I'm always smiling and I'm never in a bad mood.

I am Mr. or Mrs. Right. I always do what I "should" do, and so should you. I think nothing but pure thoughts and I always do the right thing.

I am just a weak and innocent gal and I need a big strong guy like you to take care of me.

I am strong and self-sufficient. I don't need you. I don't need anybody.

I am a big strong tough guy; I ain't afraid of anything.

I am so intelligent. Every word that comes out of my mouth drips with wisdom.

I am such a good person. See how giving and kind I am? I don't have a selfish bone in my body.

Living a false life and hiding behind facades drains our energy and saps our vitality. When your life is driven by what others think, you are no longer in control of your feelings and you are at the mercy of uncontrollable external forces. When you can accept yourself (warts and all) and understand that we are all package deals consisting of both good and bad ingredients, life becomes easier.

Whenever someone's behavior bugs you, it is usually mirroring back to you some aspect of your own personality that you have trouble accepting, parts of ourselves that we try to disown or deny. Understanding this can be a powerful feedback mechanism. If someone says something to you that is hurtful, it's probably because it has an element of truth in it. If it were completely unfounded, then it shouldn't cause you pain.

Here is a great exercise for the brave: ask your friends not only for feedback as to what they like about you, but also what they don't like about you. The negative and less flattering comments will always reflect back to you where you are not being real and accepting of yourself. Don't we all like real and authentic people rather than phony and posturing people? Posturing and maintaining a false facade is our way of denying and disowning parts of ourselves.

When I'm teaching seminars, I have to work on not playing the "the know-it-all" professor role which leads to feelings of superiority and omnipotence. This type of self-deception makes it difficult for me to be open to learning from class members. (And believe me, teaching can be a great learning experience if you provide an open, safe atmosphere and encourage questions.) Class members frequently ask thought-provoking questions that provide the stimulus for me to think deeper about a specific topic and this learning process makes for better, higher quality and more insightful seminars.

I have also discovered that when I'm in my "guru" role, it's hard for me to say "I don't know" and accept that it's not possible for me to have a ready response for every question. Acknowledging that makes me more real and allows me to connect more easily with class members.

When I made the decision to teach, counsel and write for a living, I knew that this form of service or contribution would be very fulfilling. I also attempted to accept unconditionally the notion that a life of service is all that mattered and money wasn't relevant. My wife was concerned that I had secretly taken vows of poverty. I tried to disown my baser instincts of greed and wouldn't admit to myself that I really do enjoy things that require money (e.g., traveling, dining out frequently and buying a large number of books every month). When I accepted this, I negotiated a settlement with myself between my desire to teach and help others with a healthy desire for attaining or doing other things that I really enjoy. I became more authentic and achieved a more realistic balance that makes my life work better. I have learned that teaching and financial success do not have to be mutually exclusive. Conflicting desires can pop up in any area of your life. They need to be identified, understood, resolved and accepted.

Fantasies and dark thoughts can conflict with what we feel are proper thoughts or behavior. This can cause painful shame and guilt. The reality is we all wrestle with conflicting desires and emotions. We all have our dark side, our secret thoughts that we feel would be so shaming if anyone else knew. When you try to totally repress or deny your dark side, you pay the price in unnecessary suffering.

This doesn't mean that you have to act on these thoughts, but you have to at least acknowledge that they exist and understand that just because they exist, you are not bad, evil, wicked, lecherous or the devil incarnate. It merely indicates that you are human; we all wrestle with the same emotions, thoughts and desires.

I consider myself a happily married man, but that doesn't mean I'm immune from sexual fantasies that include women other than my wife. (No good-looking woman is safe from my fantasies.) I like to think of myself as someone who loves and appreciates children, but when I'm writing and the neighborhood kids are making noise outside my window, loving thoughts are harder to achieve. Thoughts about population control and year-round schooling pop into my head. When we learn to accept our dark side life becomes easier.

Professor Oscar Ichazo summarizes the dilemma beautifully with these insights on the polarities of thought we all do battle with:

"Inside every puritan is a hedonist; inside every hedonist is a puritan; each denies the other.

Inside every confident peacock is an insecure chicken; inside every chicken is a peacock; each devalues the other.

Inside every workhorse is a lazybones; inside every lazybones is a workhorse; each secretly envies the other.

Inside each social butterfly is a lone wolf; inside each lone wolf is a social butterfly; each secretly disdains the other.

Inside every know-it-all is a questioner; inside every questioner is a know-it-all; each is impatient with the other.

Inside each skillful person is a bluffer, inside each bluffer is a skillful person; each argues with the other.

Inside each team player is a rebel; inside each rebel is a team player; each resents the other.

Inside every rigid person is a sentimentalist; inside every sentimentalist is a rigid person; each disavows the other.

Inside every believer is a doubter; inside every doubter is a believer; each rejects the other."

Growth involves identifying, understanding and integrating all these subpersonalities or polarities. The more you grow, the more real you become.

A great visualization exercise is to imagine these subpersonalities as little children. When you have conflicting feelings, hold one with each hand and allow them to have a dialogue; let each of them talk. You, being the adult, will help them work it out and search for a compromise that will work for both.

I always have to reach a compromise between my impulsive, "devil may care" subpersonality and my conservative, miserly and frugal subpersonality. One part of me says, "Wouldn't it be great fun to buy an Amtrak ticket and bum around the country for couple of months or go on a two week retreat in India?" The other part of me says, "What about the expense? Is that what you really want to do? Do you want to do that or do you want to take a vacation with Kathy and if not, why not?" This calls for a dialogue with my subpersonalities to discover what I really want. It's like saying, "OK, kids, lets stop fighting, be more grown up and work this thing out."

You don't want to have negative beliefs about any of your subpersonalities. At one time they might have been acting in your best interests and still might be trying to protect you in some way. You have to listen to them with an open mind and see what they have to say.

For me, the lesson I learned early in life was not to trust, and to fend for myself. That was valid as a child because I had two alcoholic parents. Circumstances have changed. I now have a wife that not only cares for me but also is a person that I love to travel with. So it's in my best interest to overcome my lone wolf tendencies and to trust and travel with my wife.

When I listen to all my subpersonalities, I come from a place of greater understanding and make better and healthier decisions.

Identifying, Understanding And Managing Moods

**Time cools. Time clarifies. No mood
can be maintained quite unaltered
through the course of hours.**

Thomas Mann

We all experience mood swings. Some mood swings are slight (temporary excitements and disappointments); other mood swings are large and more significant (manic-depressive behavior). We never seem to be in one place emotionally for long. Just when it seems like life is going smoothly, bam, our mood level drops and life again seems rocky. Or just when life seems hopeless, our mood lifts and all seems right again.

When you are in a good mood, life seems good and everything is manageable. When you are in a bad mood, your coping skills are overwhelmed and nothing seems to work smoothly. Our moods are always fluctuating. The trap that needs to be avoided is believing that life has suddenly become significantly worse or better in the past day or the last hour. It's our perspective and outlook that has changed.

As an individual humorously said in counseling, "You know, when the Minnesota Vikings win, my wife is good company and a lot of fun to be around, but when they lose, she is so stupid and doesn't understand anything. Although she never watches football and visits her mom when the game is on, it really is amazing how the outcome of a football game transforms my wife." Obviously the wife hasn't changed; the husband's perspective and mood has changed.

Moods come and go. I have learned to be grateful for the good moods and to patiently wait out the bad moods, knowing that they will change. It's not possible to identify and manage all the variables that trigger mood swings. PMS can cause mood swings in women. Dietary imbalances, inclement weather, absence of light (Seasonal Affective Disorder), negative people and experiences and excessive worry, to name a few, affect many people.

We can learn methods to help maximize good moods and minimize bad moods. The first step is gaining awareness of the risk factors that can trigger your mood swings. Here is my list of things I do to prevent bad moods:

When I wake up, I immediately get up and start moving around (usually in the direction of the kitchen for that first cup of coffee). My system needs a little caffeine in the morning, but not too much or I get wired and pay the price later on in the day when I come down from a caffeine high. After a little experimenting, I've discovered that 3 cups of a blend of 1/2 caffeine and 1/2 decaffeinated coffee works just fine.

I pay close attention as to how my day begins. The way the first hour of the day goes, so goes the day. If I get off to a good start, I usually have a good day. If I get off to a bad start, I have a tendency to procrastinate and goof off. Wasting time is never inspirational.

It's impossible for me be in a bad mood on a sunny day. Cloudy overcast days are slippery emotional slopes for me and I'm susceptible to mild grade depression. My strategy for gloomy days is to be active, avoid negative people and to guard against too much thinking and over analyzing.

Minnesotans have long winters to endure. Long cold winters coupled with stressful holiday seasons are real risk factors. Kathy and I always take a vacation during December or January. This renews us and gives us the energy and outlook to hang in there until spring.

Mood swings are inevitable; they come and they go. It's like the weather in Minnesota, if you don't like it, wait a little while and it will change.

We have discussed possible remedies or preventive maintenance to help you sidestep bad moods. Unfortunately, no matter how hard you work on avoiding people and situations that trigger or alter moods, you will still occasionally find yourself in low moods. It always helps to have awareness of mood shifts. When you are in a bad mood, you need to fine-tune your daily living strategies.

Life looks so serious when we are in a bad or low mood. The same behavior by our spouse and friends can be endearing when we are in a good mood and can be annoying and bothersome when we are in a bad mood. This is one of real destructive forces in relationships. There is a much higher probability that we will say hurtful things that are never forgotten and can really damage relations when we are in a bad mood.

The lesson to be learned is to develop awareness of our

moods and when in a low or bad mood don't tackle relationship issues. This is confusing because that is the exact time that we want to confront other people and solve problems. When we are in a bad mood, we want to get to the bottom of something, we want to express feelings, and be assertive and defend our boundaries.

Develop the discipline to learn to discuss relationship issues when you are in a good mood rather than a bad mood. The probabilities of success are far greater. It also helps to understand your partner's mood. Wait until you are both in a good mood to work on relationship issues; this provides an even greater probability of success.

Focus

**A life devoted to trifles not only takes
away the inclination, but the capacity,
for higher pursuits.**

Hannah More

We all understand the importance of knowing what you want and setting goals to help you achieve your objectives. Learning how to focus is a powerful strategy that makes accomplishing objectives easier and more enjoyable. Avoid and eliminate all the distractions that stall and derail you.

Time wasters always seem to pop up when we begin to undertake a new challenge or struggle to make progress on existing projects. When I sit down to write, it's easy to find "fun" time wasters. The TV is just a click away. The computer offers all kinds of options to do anything but what I really intended to do when I logged on. I can play hearts, solitaire, read my email, surf the Internet or check out the stock markets.

I have devised some rules that help me keep focused on the task at hand:

1) When I decide to undertake a new project, I develop a plan that describes what I want to accomplish, why and the process that will help me achieve my

goal. I keep that plan handy and refer to it frequently. This makes me refocus on my goals by reinforcing and reminding myself of all the benefits. It's fun to achieve; it's not fun to dawdle, procrastinate and waste time. My plan is a working document; nothing is etched in stone. If I discover a way to improve the original plan, I modify it accordingly.

2) Everyday I ask myself a couple of questions to tighten my focus on what needs to be done:

a) What is the single most important thing I must do to keep myself on the path to realize my goal or objective?

b) What is the one thing I can do today to advance towards my goal or objective?

3) I always am looking to refine and enhance my procedures and systems. Good procedures allow us to handle the necessary mundane things without wasting energy that could be channeled into the more creative and exciting aspects of our work. Much of what we do is repetitive and routine. Woody Allen once said that 90% of success is just showing up. I think a large part of success is just doing the routine things that need to be done. Success is 10% inspiration and 90% perspiration. Establishing successful routines is a significant factor in becoming a competent and achieving person.

There is a strong correlation between establishing good systems and attaining success in achieving goals. If your are disorganized, you will waste time and energy. Here are some tips that you might wish to consider:

a) Elimination of clutter – Clutter is a symptom of being unorganized.

For a writer, collecting information is half the battle. Labeling and filing it for later reference and use is equally important. Scraps of paper containing scribbled notes strewn all over the house constitutes a bad case of clutter for a writer.

I can really empathize with squirrels who have buried nuts for the winter, but when winter comes they haven't a clue where they are buried. Clutter dampens your spirits and creates frustration rather than creative joyous energy. Nothing drains my energy more than searching for a misplaced object or wasting time looking for misfiled information.

b) Create a workspace that's enjoyable and conducive to creativity.

I like to have easy access to supplies, materials, reference books, computer files and my coffee cup. I also value comfortable furniture (a quality computer chair), an ergonomic computer set up (a large monitor at the proper eye level, a trackball mouse to prevent carpal tunnel syndrome).

Good lighting is essential. You want a setting that is not only pleasing to the eye, but also good for the spirits. Your workspace should have an ambiance that naturally draws you to it.

c) Minimize distractions.

Learn to anticipate and sidestep distractions. At the end of the workday, ask yourself these questions concerning distractions and uninvited intrusions into your daily work routine:

What were my major distractions today?

How long did it take me to recover? (Often a 5-minute distraction will require a large amount of time to resolve and you are no longer in synch with the original task before the interruption.) If you have to ask yourself, "Now where was I?" your train of thought has been broken.

Were the distractions and interruptions avoidable?

What might I have done differently today?

d) Commit to regularly scheduled daily action.
    To me, this is the secret of all progress. When I'm willing to commit to daily action, I know it just a matter of time before I achieve my goal, and that's a wonderful feeling.

Focused people are highly efficient people.

The Ultimate Freedom: Choice

A happy person is not someone to whom "bad" things do not happen. Rather, it is someone who understands that his or her reactions to events are the stuff of happiness.

Alan Epstein

You are everything you choose to be. One of the real keys to happiness and serenity is the realization and understanding that you always have a choice. Every waking conscious moment provides you with the opportunity of choice. When you forget or haven't the awareness of options and choices, you begin to suffer and create a victim's mentality.

Victims feel powerless because they feel they have no choices. With no choice, there can be no change. Without the possibility of change, there is no hope. Without hope, we feel stuck, paralyzed and helpless. Gaining real power is permitting yourself to create more choices and options. When you develop the awareness that you always have choices, you understand that you have control over your life.

Let's take a worst case scenario to see if choice still exists. Everyone would agree that the holocaust experience suffered by the Jews in World War Two is about as inconceivably horrific as it gets, and yet choice still existed. Author Victor Frankl recounts in *Man's Search For Meaning* choosing humor to lessen the suffering. He and a friend promised each other to invent at least one humorous story daily, about some incident that could happen one day after their liberation. When they were on a train being transported to a concentration camp, they chose a joyous response in discovering that the train was not heading for the Mauthausen camp, "only" for Dachau.

Frankl also recounted stories of inmates who chose compassion over selfishness by walking through the camp comforting others and giving away their last piece of bread.

Frankl concluded from his concentration camp experience that everything can be taken from a man but one thing: the last of the human freedoms - to choose one's attitude in any given set of circumstances, to choose one's own way.

One of the major complaints I hear is that there is so much to do and so little time. I gently remind people that we are all working under the same constraints when it comes to time. It's really a matter of choices on how to live your life and spend your time (priorities and good time management skills).

One of the most powerful choices you can make is learning to say no, not only to people but also to time wasting activities and things you really don't want to do. The more you permit yourself the choice to say no, the more control you have over your life. Saying no isn't easy, but it's a learned skill and with practice it becomes easier. I have great respect for those who can say no to a dinner party invitation without feeling obligated to justify their decision with a transparent excuse ("I'll take a raincheck" or "Gee, I'm busy that night"), when the truth is that it's simply something they have chosen not to do. Saying "no" shouldn't be viewed as an act of unkindness, but as an act of integrity necessary for your personal well being. Integrity means that your behavior is consistent with your values and beliefs.

Individuals make choices about how happily or unhappily married they are. I have chosen (and so has my wife) to be happily married. Kathy and I went to four different marriage counselors looking for insights to make our marriage work. We knew if we could make it work, it would be a great marriage. Traditional marriage counseling provided no answers. One counselor stressed the need for better communication skills. That wasn't the problem. We both are very clear that we are somewhat selfish (not necessarily a bad thing) and we really prefer to have the other see and do it our way. This hasn't changed, but we have learned to accept and appreciate each other and to negotiate the differences. We both believe our differences are good for the relationship.

A light bulb moment for me was after coming home from the final emotionally charged session with the last counselor. My longhaired cat "Peaches" met me at the door. Peaches sheds hair over all the furniture, frequently regurgitates hairballs and will occasionally bite you if you don't immediately begin petting her when she jumps uninvited into your lap. I'm very fond of my cat and understand that these behaviors and inconveniences come with the territory of owning a longhaired, crotchety cat. Peaches and I have never been in therapy. It's all about acceptance.

If I choose to be in a relationship with Kathy, I have to accept who she is, how she communicates, her values and her life style.

One of my core beliefs is that happiness is really an inside job. Others can't make you feel happy, good and at peace with yourself. Good relationships are a great perk in life, but the key to real happiness is the relationship one has with one's self.

I think it's an oversold myth that the key to successful marriages is finding the right person. There are thousands of right people for you, if you don't need to be overly and neurotically dependent upon your spouse for your happiness. It's not finding the right person; it's being the right person. After I decided to be happily married and understood that Kathy could be a great partner in a wonderful relationship, I begun to make other choices to support my choice to be happily married. I chose to focus on what's good about the relationship rather than what's lacking in the relationship. Kathy is a highly independent woman, who travels extensively and leads a full and exciting life. This provides me the space and solitude my highly introverted personality requires and freedom to pursue my own interests. I really enjoy being married to a high energy, on-the-go person. I also enjoy my wife's companionship. I understand I can't have it both ways; someone who loves to travel and has many friends and social obligations cannot be at home 7 days a week, cooking meals and entertaining me. I chose to feel fortunate rather than deprived, to be in a relationship with such a dynamic and interesting person.

I chose to work strictly on my own issues and not try to fix my wife. I have discovered the more I work on myself (being more loving and practicing deeper listening) the better she gets. I chose to be supportive of my wife's goals rather than selfishly demand that she subordinate her desires and be subservient to me in any form. I always miss my wife when she travels but her happiness is more important to me than her feeling obligated or burdened by our relationship. I chose to act in a way is best for the relationship. The criteria for a good relationship isn't right vs. wrong, but whether a particular action or behavior creates intimacy and trust rather than distancing and alienation.

I have also chosen to love my kids and not let them drive me crazy. I no longer allow myself to be set up for disappointment by what I view as thoughtless or immature behavior. After several scheduled visits in which one of my kids forgot and wouldn't be at home to meet me, we now meet in a coffee shop of a large bookstore. If he shows up, I'm delighted. If he forgets, I have no problem killing time in a bookstore.

Having a bad attitude or a good attitude is a choice.

Which set of people gets more enjoyment out of life: those with a chip on their shoulder or those with a good attitude?

Personal growth is a choice. Real growth requires you to make the choice to be honest with yourself and choose to build into your schedule time to reflect and work on your issues. It requires soul searching and honest introspection to identify root causes, bad habits and previously made poor choices.

If you can learn to question rather than blindly accept, you will discover the multitude of choices that are available to you:

How do you spend your time? What activities are done by default rather than for real enjoyment? Do you engage in meaningless arguments, discussion and debates? Do you routinely and mindlessly watch boring television shows?

Who do you talk to and associate with? Are your friends nurturing and supportive or are they anchors around you neck? Do they inspire you and make you feel good or does their negativity depress and pull you down?

What makes you angry?

What time do you get up in the morning?

How do you choose to look and present yourself to the world?

How do you choose to deal with problems?

What do you expect from yourself?

How do you choose to deal with others?

Do you choose to coast through life following the path of least resistance?

Do you choose to set goals?

After making a big or major choice, we can make smaller choices that support the larger choice. For example:

Major choice - The Choice To Lose Weight

Supporting Choices

> The choice to eat the right kind and
> amount of food.
> The choice to exercise.
> The choice to avoid situations and people
> that encourage poor eating habits.
> The choice to spend more time with
> people who encourage and support
> your weight-loss choice.
> The choice to educate yourself about
> nutrition and better eating habits.
> The choice to have greater awareness and
> selectivity when shopping.
> The choice to say no to second helpings
> or dessert.

Major Choice - The Choice To Improve An Important Personal Relationship

Supporting Choices

> The choice to be more loving.
> The choice to learn and practice better
> listening skills.

The choice to express yourself more
positively.
The choice to accept and not blame or
shame.
The choice to work on cooperation.
The choice to eliminate hurtful arguments
and learn to disagree respectfully.
The choice to find more common
interests to share.

Major Choice - The Choice To Get More Accomplished

Supporting Choices

The choice to have written goals.
The choice to focus and eliminate
distractions.
The choice to make and follow a plan.
The choice to ask for help when needed.
The choice to discover and utilize
available resources.
The choice to take breaks for purposes of
renewal.
The choice to reward yourself for
accomplishments.

Success is a culmination of a series of minor choices. Your have to exercise your right to choose in order to provide yourself with the benefits of change. Your future is wholly determined by the choices you are currently making. Manage your choices and you will control the direction of your life

Choices are available to all in every facet of their life. The following list of questions is provided to raise your level of awareness about the endless number of choices that are available to you. You might choose to spend a few minutes reviewing the list and note the choices that you think might be applicable and beneficial to you. Ask yourself - do you think there are choices you could make which would improve your life?

Do I have the courage to name what I want?

Do I have written goals?

Do I go after what I want?

Am I willing to learn new skills?

Am I willing to pay attention and learn better listening skills?

Do I allow small and inconsequential things to bother me?

Do I exercise good personal grooming habits?
  Are my fingernails always clean and
    trimmed?
  Do I get a hair cut on a regular basis?
  Are my shoes shined?
  Do I change my socks and underwear
    daily?

Do I try to lead a clutter free existence?
  Do I keep my car clean and free of trash?
  Do I either fix up promptly or throw
    away broken items?

Do I procrastinate?

Am I willing to examine my life and ask myself

hard questions?

Am I willing to work on my personal growth?

Is there anything I can do to lead a healthier
lifestyle?

When and where do I eat out?
How often do I eat out?

How much TV do I watch?
What programs do I choose to watch on TV?

How much do I read?
What types of books do I read?
Do I read newspapers?
Do I read magazines?
Do I subscribe to magazines?
Do I go to the movies?
What types of movies do I see?

Do I write letters?
Do I write emails?
Do I write thank you notes?

Do I have hobbies?
Do I make time for my hobbies?

Do I maintain a good personal image?
    What type of clothes do I wear?
    Do I wear appropriate clothing for
        various outings?
    Do I wear a hat?
    Do I wear a hat backwards?

Do I take advantage of the latest technology?
    Do I own a cell phone?
    Do I own a computer?
    Do I keep my computer skills up to date?

Am I willing to take risks?

Am I willing to experiment?

Am I willing to learn how to cook new dishes?

What time do I get up?

What time do I go to bed?

Do I vote?

Am I financially responsible?
    Do I save money on a regular basis?
    Do I invest a portion of my income?
    Do I promptly pay monthly credit card
    bills to avoid interest charges?

Do I drink?

Who do I listen to and whose advice do I follow?

Do I give unsolicited and unwanted advice?

How much do I socialize?

How much time do I have for myself?

How do I celebrate holidays?

How do I show my spouse or significant other that

I love him or her?

Do I give presents?
When?
To Whom?
How much am I willing to spend?

Do I send Christmas or holiday cards?

How do I nurture myself?

How do I celebrate life's victories?

Do I give compliments?

Do I ever perform random acts of kindness?

Do I smile?
How often?
How genuine?

Do I approach and talk to strangers?

Do I tell lies?

Do I habitually complain?

Am I supportive of others?

Do I start the day off with a healthy breakfast?

Do I own a pet?

Where do I shop?
Do I comparison shop?

What type of people do I associate with?

What do I think about when I wake up?

What do I think about when I go to bed at night?

Do I spend time outside on nice days?
  Do I take walks?
  Do I watch sunsets?
  Do I watch sunrises?

Do I share?

Do I dwell excessively on things that happened in the past?

Do I fantasize excessively about the future?

Do I have dreams?
  Am I willing to take action?
  Am I willing to take a first step?

Do I worry excessively?

People who do not identify their choices live by default and forfeit control over their future.

Questions

**Life will give you what you ask
of her if only you ask long
enough and plainly enough.**

Edith Nesbit

One of the best strategies for self-improvement is learning to ask the right questions as illustrated in the following story:

A fellow, new in town, wanted to get acquainted with local folks, so he walked over to the village square and saw an old-timer on a bench. Tied to the bench next to him was a rather mean-looking German shepherd. The stranger looked at the dog tentatively and asked, "Does your dog bite?" The old-timer said "Nope." So the stranger reached down to pet him. The dog lunged at him and tried to take off his arm. Quick reaction saved his arm but not his coat. Looking at his shredded coat sleeve, the stranger turned to the old timer and said, " I thought you said your dog doesn't bite." The old timer replied "It ain't my dog".

We are always talking to ourselves. We constantly evaluate and question what we have done and what we plan to do. Questions define your focus and that determines what you think. Your thoughts will determine how you feel and feelings dictate whether you take positive action or act indecisively and do less. If you want to change the quality of your life, change the kinds of questions you habitually ask yourself.

Learning to ask empowering questions helps us focus on possibilities rather than problems. People who enjoy and live life well, ask better questions and as a result get better answers. Quality questions lead to a quality life. Disempowering questions focus on what is wrong rather than what's right. People who consistently ask themselves disempowering questions guarantee themselves negative, discouraging feelings.

Here are some typical disempowering questions that people ask themselves:

> Why am I a loser?
> Why doesn't anybody like me?
> Why am I so unlucky?

Take a little test. Ask yourself one of these three questions and evaluate how you feel. Consider how you would consistently feel and view life if you habitually asked that question.

Disempowering questions lead to feelings of resignation and hopelessness. No good feelings ever emanate from them.

The subconscious doesn't censor or discriminate; it merely processes. It doesn't say, "that's an unhealthy question for you to be asking yourself;" it automatically begins to search your memory banks and looks for data that is consistent with the question. If you ask a disempowering question, the mind will dredge up disempowering answers. If you were always asking yourself "Why can't I ever get ahead in life?" your mind will accommodate you and feed back to you all the negative, disempowering data it can find to answer the question. Every shaming experience, every perceived defect will be found and served up to you. Answers like "because you are stupid, because you don't deserve to, because you don't have the proper education, because you don't know the right people, because you are a born loser, because nobody really likes you" will pop into your consciousness. Disempowering questions always lead to disempowering answers. Any area of your life can be diminished by disempowering questions.

Marriages and other long-term relationships are either damaged or improved by how we view the relationship and the questions we ask ourselves about the relationship. I have listed and categorized questions that people frequently ask about their relationships:

Disempowering questions:

Is this the best I can do?

Why did I marry such a loser?

Why is he/she so _____ (you fill in the blank - selfish, sloppy stupid etc.)?

Empowering questions:

How can I improve this relationship?

How can I show more love towards my spouse or partner?

What do I really like about my spouse or partner?

How can we help each other to grow and enjoy life?

Questions about work can also be categorized:

Disempowering:

> Why doesn't anybody appreciate me
> around here?

> Why do I have to work with a bunch of
> idiots?

Empowering:

> What needs to be done around here and
> what can I do to help?

> How can I do my job better?

> What constructive things can I do to
> advance my career?

What you will discover is that there are never good answers to disempowering questions; there are always good answers to empowering questions.

Begin to examine all areas of your life and locate where empowering questions can help you. You might discover powerful questions that can really assist you in getting unstuck and moving forward. I have two favorites: "What is the one thing I can do today to help me achieve my goals and realize my dreams?" When I stumble or have a setback, I ask myself "How can I learn from this problem so that it won't happen in the future?"

Questions immediately change our focus and therefore change how we feel. Asking yourself "What are my fondest memories?" or "What am I truly grateful for?" will create warm and pleasant feelings. We can control how we feel by habitually asking ourselves good questions. "What am I excited about or optimistic about in my life now?" is a question that forces you to focus in a positive way.

Asking yourself "What was the worst day of my life?" or "Why was my childhood so terrible?" can only create unpleasant feelings. If you choose to stay stuck in a really painful emotional state, ask yourself questions that create a feeling of helplessness. "How could you do this terrible thing to me?" or "Why is my life so messed up?" or "Why is there so much pain and suffering in the world?"

Questions can either make us aware of or blind to the resources that are available to us. Questions alter our perceptions of who we are, what we capable of achieving and how we feel. Be wary of asking limiting questions; limiting questions hamstring your imagination. A crippled imagination damages your creative powers and prevents you from considering all the wonderful possibilities of life.

Asking empowering question doesn't guarantee that the best answer will instantaneously appear, but if you persist in asking a good answer you will eventually get an answer that will work for you. Good questions will lead to other good questions and puts you on the right path to discovering the answer that is best for you.

Asking empowering questions is a powerful strategy to help you change your life. This strategy can be refined by formulating a series of questions that address an issue on which progress needs to be made. Anthony Robbins in *Awaken The Giant Within* discusses the use of questions to create a problem solving state. Here is how I used that strategy to work on my financial well being:

Issue: I was not feeling financially secure. What could I do to create wealth and to have a healthy relationship with money?

Question #1: What are the lessons I can learn from my current situation?

I didn't know. This first answer didn't feel like a helpful answer, so I continued to ask the question until I found an answer that contributed to the solution. The answer that worked was that I have finally developed the maturity and honesty to acknowledge to myself that this is an issue I needed to work on.

Question #2: What was I willing change?
Several good answers and insights surfaced. I needed to live on a budget, set financial goals, accept personal responsibility for my financial life and change my attitude about money. I also decided that denial of this issue was something that needed to be addressed.

I also needed to cease trying to convince Kathy that my philosophy about money was right and hers was wrong; this shift in attitude created more intimacy in our relationship rather than constant conflict.

Question #3 - How can I enjoy the process while I do what is necessary to change?
I learned that I can enjoy creating an ambitious plan and posting progress to it and that it's comforting to know that I can control my financial destiny and eliminate worry.

Examine all areas of your life and identify places where you feel stuck and would like to make progress.

If you are a slow starter in the morning, construct a series of questions that will put you in an optimistic mood and raise your energy level:

What are the things in life that are bringing me

happiness?

What are some of the things that I am thankful for in my life now?

How can I use my unique talents to help and bring happiness to other people?

What can I do today to help myself realize my dreams?

You can end the day on a good note by asking a series of questions that helps you review the day's events in a positive way.

What positive lessons in life did I learn today?

How did I contribute today?

How can I make tomorrow an even better day?

What did I accomplish today that makes me feel good?

If you are undertaking a new challenge in life, develop a series of questions that can assist you in learning what you need to know to be successful:

What skills do I need to master?

What knowledge do I need to acquire?

What attitudes do I want to develop?

What new feelings, convictions, and values do I want to cultivate?

What goals do I need to establish?

What resources do I need?

What resources are available to me?

A series of questions can be constructed to help you in the develop better personal awareness:

How have I successfully solved my problems in the past?

What types of challenges do I enjoy?

What types of questions can I ask myself that provide me meaningful answers?

What are my strengths and weaknesses?

What are my natural talents?

Where and when in the past have I been successful and how can I use that to ensure success in the future?

What motivates and inspires me?

What kind of work and accomplishment makes me feel fulfilled?

Empowering questions will provide positive answers that can motivate and inspire you to take action and alters your emotional state in a positive life affirming way.

Does What You Believe
Help You Or Harm You?

We don't see things as they are.
We see things as we are.

Anais Nin

The basic principles and rules of living can be confusing. Because children lack experience and judgement, we are taught spiritual principles and rules as absolutes. Something is right or wrong, good or bad. In school, answers are correct or incorrect.

There are some guiding spiritual principles that you may feel *are* absolutes and that the more consistent you live your life abiding by these principles the better your life will work. As an example, I believe in unconditional love. I accept that the more I practice unconditional love the better my life will work. I also understand I'm a flawed human and will never attain total mastery or perfection.

Viewing *everything* in black and white, absolutist terms is a hard way to go through life; it makes for a difficult journey. A better approach is understand that you never know all there is to know and have a willingness to be open to new information and fresh perspectives. Accept that total clarity is not always possible. Many rules for living effectively are relative. Context often determines appropriateness. The challenge is to balance and reconcile these conflicting guidelines. If I were to ask you if killing people was a bad thing, an immoral thing, you would probably say yes, absolutely. But then if I were to ask you about self-defense and point out to you that people are given medals for killing in wartime, the question becomes more difficult to answer. The realm of truth becomes a little murkier.

What needs to be addressed is where you are living arbitrarily and rigidly by a set of rules that really have no spiritual underpinning, where you are living unconsciously and adhering to unquestioned and unexamined beliefs. The $64,000 question you need to ask yourself concerning each belief is whether it is empowering (good for you) or disempowering (bad for you). This is why awareness plays such an important role in personal development.

Next it is necessary to have effective strategies for eliminating or revising beliefs that harm or limit you. Why is this so critical? Whatever you are feeling or experiencing is usually preceded by a thought. If you are experiencing a positive emotion and are feeling good, loving or confident, this feeling has been preceded by a positive thought. If you are experiencing some negative emotion (fear, anger, feeling of inadequacy, depression etc.) you have probably been having a corresponding negative thought. Thoughts precede feelings and feelings precede action (or lack of action). The sequence of events is beliefs, thoughts, feelings, and action.

Here is an example. Let's say you are single and your social life is languishing. You find yourself sitting home alone on too many Friday nights. Although you know you aren't going to meet Mr. or Mrs. Right traveling from the couch to the refrigerator, you can't seem to break the pattern. If you have thoughts such as "I'm overweight and nobody will find me attractive" or "I'm too old" or "There is nobody out there for me," what emotions and feelings will this kind of thinking trigger? You will probably feel either down, depressed, angry, frustrated, upset or some combination of these feelings. What actions will this negative feeling trigger? Probably inaction; you will want to stay at home and do nothing. If you had positive thoughts, positive beliefs, you would feel better and would have a higher probability of taking some type of action that would change a pattern that isn't working for you.

Personal growth requires that you develop the awareness of identifying your disempowering thoughts and learn methods to create empowering thoughts. Empowering thoughts lead to good feelings and good feelings are the springboard for positive action.

Affirmations

**A person's mind stretched by a new idea
can never return to its original dimension.**

Oliver Wendell Holmes

A very powerful thought altering strategy is the use of affirmations. Affirmations will help you increase your enthusiasm, boost your confidence, get control over your emotions and bolster your self-esteem.

The use of affirmations in personal growth and self-empowerment was invaluably propelled forward with the work of Doctor Emile Coue in Geneva in 1895. People in his clinic were recovering 5 times faster than the norm for other hospitals and clinics. He taught his patients to say, "Every day in every way, I'm feeling better." The doctor and nurses would also use positive feedback and greet the patients saying "Every day, in every way, you are looking better and better."

Repetition and re-enforcement is what makes affirmations work. A good program for affirmations is to say them 3 times a day; early in the morning and late at night, when you are more receptive to the power of suggestion, and once during the middle of the day.

Some enthusiasts recommend saying affirmations 1,000

times a day. That's a very powerful program but it also has a very high dropout rate.

I want to describe someone to you to help you understand the power of affirmations. I'm proud to tell you that I'm describing Kathy, my wife:

Beautiful smile
Warm, wonderful, genuine laugh
Very generous and feeling person
Possesses an incredibly high level of energy
    and passion for living
Tremendous sense of humor
    Could be a stand up comedian
    Been asked to develop and do talks on humor
Accomplished pianist- worked in piano bars
An authority on Broadway musicals
    Periodically does radio shows on musicals
Renowned and respected children's librarian
    Nominated for librarian of the year
Master's degree
Gifted speaker on numerous subjects and always
    in demand
Artistically talented
    Quilt maker
    Cake decorator
    Doll maker
    Seamstress
Loves to travel.
    Frequent trips all over the United States. Also has
    vacationed in England 7 times, Italy twice and
    France once.
Co-founded the Maud Hart Lovelace literary society
    three years ago. It currently has 600 members.
Co-authored the book - *Gotcha (Nonfiction Booktalks*
    To Get Kids Excited About Reading).
Been interviewed on numerous radio/TV shows.

Several people have wanted to publish a
book on her life story.
Has been the principal speaker at numerous
fashion shows for Nordstrom throughout the
country.

Now I'm telling you this for a reason. Doesn't Kathy
sound like she has something going for her? Don't you think
there might have been one or two men out there who had
some interest in Kathy? Kathy didn't start dating until she
was in her early forties, because Kathy had convinced herself
that no man would find her attractive. It's a self-fulfilling
prophecy; once you believe something you will take the
necessary action to make it come true.

Whenever I tell this story in one of my *Dare To Date*
seminars, I can see the wheels turning and can guess what
the men are thinking - Yea, but what did she look like? Trust
me! This wasn't an issue.

Groucho Marx once said " I wouldn't want to belong to
any club that would have me as a member". My wife would
say to herself that she wouldn't want to go out with any man
who had such bad taste as to ask her. With intensive
counseling, she shed her negative self-image and replaced it
with a much more positive self-image. Affirmations were
one of the tools she used to create a positive belief system
about herself. Kathy's favorite affirmation is the following
one:

I AM VIBRANTLY HEALTHY AND RADIANTLY
BEAUTIFUL. I AM IRRESISTIBLY ATTRACTIVE
TO MEN

Did it work? It transformed how Kathy saw herself, how she
dressed and how she interacted with men. Kathy got married
after meeting and dating 107 men over a 4-year period. I'm
the lucky guy that married Kathy. In my *Dare To Date* class, I

give Kathy's favorite affirmation to the women and I recommend the following affirmation for men:

> I AM AN ATTRACTIVE, HEALTHY AND
> INTERESTING MAN. WOMEN FIND IT EASY
> TO TALK TO ME.

Here are some additional affirmations:

> I deserve the best in life.
> Life is fun and pleasurable.
> I am responsible for creating my life.
> I am capable and competent.
> I can take care of myself.
> I deserve happiness and joy in my life.
> I can change my behavior when I need to.
> I can do anything I believe I can.
> I can create my life with my thoughts.
> I am the source of my power. My thoughts, words,
>   imagination and beliefs are my power.
> I accept and believe in prosperity for myself.
> I am worthy of prosperity.
> I am worthy of joy.
> I am worthy of happiness.
> I am friendly, outgoing and confident.
> I take complete responsibility for my life.
> My life is getting easier and happier every day.
> I am becoming more and more focused everyday.
> I am a success in all that I do.
> I am free to be myself.
> I am a highly creative individual.
> I am free to choose the direction of my life.
> I am at peace with myself.

Identify the specific issue that you wish to work on and find or create the appropriate affirmations to support the change you wish to make.

These are my criteria for choosing affirmations:

Affirmations have to have some credibility. If you are unemployed or "between engagements" and your affirmation is "I'm going to be a billionaire in 3 months", I don't care how many times you say it, it's probably not going to work for you because it lacks credibility. However, if your affirmation was "I am going to have a job in 3 months and be able to pay my bills and have a little left over to enjoy myself"; I think that has the necessary credibility to assist you in finding a job.

An affirmation should make you feel good when you say it. If it doesn't, it's too big of a stretch at that point in your life. Play with the wording and when you find that which makes you feel good, it's a good affirmation for you.

When you begin to see the power of affirmations to reprogram you in a positive way and begin to believe in their power, you will want to try new affirmations. I am a big believer in affirmations, I have them scotch-taped on my bathroom mirror, displayed on my corkboard bulletin board in the bathroom, filed in my wallet, and present in my work place. I know they work.

After you experience using affirmations in a formal program (saying them each day at the same time and the same number of times), you will begin to believe in the use of informal affirmations. Two of mine are:

I'm happily married and lucky to have Kathy in my life.

Isn't life great in the 20th century?

I say these to myself randomly throughout the day and guess what! I'm happily married and life is great for me.

Surprise

You have to have fun!
Otherwise life is like one long
dental appointment.

Debbie Fields

One of my favorite stories is about a woman waiting to board a plane at the airport. She had bought some chocolate chip cookies and decided she needed something to drink. She got up, leaving her luggage and cookies, and went for coffee. When she returned, she discovered a rather seedy looking gentleman seated next to her possessions and eating chocolate chip cookies. She was really upset. "The nerve of this bum," she thought. She angrily reached into the bag and grabbed a cookie. The old man smiled and reached into the bag and also retrieved a cookie. This went on until there was only one cookie left. The old man retrieved the final cookie broke it in half and offered half to the young lady. She was absolutely furious; the unmitigated gall of this old geezer.

She boarded the plane, still visibly upset, sat down and reached into her carry-on bag for a magazine and discovered a bag of unopened cookies. The old man was sharing his cookies, not hers! We now see the cast of characters in a different light.

You never know all there is to know about a situation.

Being open to the possibility of additional information will make you less judgmental, less rigid, and allows an easier shifting of perspectives. Intransigent people are stuck. Being stuck doesn't allow growth.

Modeling

**Action may not always bring happiness;
but there is no happiness without action.**

Benjamin Disraeli

There are many ways to learn. I think a balanced approach using multiple strategies is best. I love to read, but reading is a passive activity and is only one way to learn. You could read some excellent books on public speaking, but it would not be as beneficial as joining Toastmasters and practicing.

There is nothing as real and transforming as doing the actual experience. Participation and practicing what you want to master is probably the most effective learning method.. Michael Jordan didn't become a star and arguably the greatest ever to play the game of basketball by reading books on basketball.

Don't limit yourself by allowing reading to be your only method of learning. That approach creates a lot of highly intelligent but underperforming people. They fail to go from insight to action. They think and anticipate but never leave the sidelines. Reading should be one component in an integrated approach.

Another effective strategy for learning is modeling: a

process in which we copy or duplicate someone's behavior and belief systems in order to achieve the same results. It's a powerful way to accelerate the learning process when compared to the traditional trial and error method of learning. We can model those behaviors of people who have had success in areas that we wish to emulate.

My wife is my role model in so many ways; she leads an incredibly full life and accomplishes so much. I've have always battled procrastination and had a tendency to "skate through life" and do only what was necessary to get by. Unfortunately my belief when I was in school was that anything over a "C" was overkill. I had programmed myself for mediocrity.

Kathy's approach seemed so much more fulfilling and joyous. I wanted to learn how to add more zest and joy to life. I started observing and modeling her behavior. The first step was to gain an understanding of her belief system, which is the underpinning of her fulfilling life. Obviously these were empowering beliefs for Kathy and I believed they would also be beneficial for me. Kathy believes:

YOU SHOULD BE THE BEST YOU CAN BE

LIFE IS NOT A DRESS REHEARSAL - We only get one opportunity and we need to make the most of it. Live every day and make every moment count.

TIME IS NOT A RENEWABLE COMMODITY - Financial losses can be recouped, but time poorly spent and wasted is gone forever.

I begun to observe her behavior in detail and I identified patterns that are supportive and consistent with her belief systems.

Kathy jumps up (no contemplation or turning over for

another 15 minutes in bed) at 5:30 every morning. She makes a pot of coffee the night before and sets the coffee pot timer so that she is greeted with the aroma of a freshly brewed pot of coffee when she enters the kitchen.

This leaping out of bed stuff felt unnatural to me, so I gave myself a little out, a little wriggle room. I told myself that I could always go back to bed if I chose to. I very seldom exercise that option.

Kathy never procrastinates. If a decision needs to be made, she makes it. If something need to be done, she does it. I was the type that would con myself into saying I'll play in the morning and do those chores in the afternoon (mow the grass, put up the screens etc.). Then when afternoon came, I would invariably want to play more and put off the chores until the next day.

Procrastination is such an energy drainer. Although you might be putting off the actual chore, you add one more item to your mental list of unfinished things that need to be done and this list is always in your consciousness, diverting your thoughts and eroding your energy. The lower your rate of procrastination, the higher your level of energy.

Kathy falls into a deep sleep within 5 minutes after going to bed. I was really envious of this. I sleep poorly and never fall immediately asleep. Kathy has learned to power down just like a computer being turn off. How does Kathy do this?

TAKES A WARM BATH BEFORE GOING TO BED

DOES LIGHT READING BEFORE TAKING THE BATH

WILL NOT DISCUSS HEAVY ISSUES LATE AT NIGHT

Kathy rewards herself for good performance and completed tasks. Kathy does a lot of public speaking and when she give a particularly good speech, she rewards herself with a bubble bath and allows herself to be rubbed down (that's my job) with Vita Spa lotion. (After average speeches she just gets an ordinary lotion.)

Being a librarian, she loves to read and after completing various tasks (e.g., 2 hours data entry on the computer), she allows herself to read for a 1/2 hour.

Kathy is never without her personal planner/organizer and all scheduling and plans are logged in. Once you learn to write everything down, energy is no longer wasted trying to remember details. The use of a planner is essential for the busy person. It frees up your mind for other more productive and creative types of thinking.

Kathy searches for ways to be more productive and eliminate "time wasters." We upgraded our computer system to reduce the time required for software to be loaded and ready for use. All trips up and down the stairs to our apartment are multi-purpose. No special trips just to take out the garbage. Kathy has no mercy or compassion for phone solicitors - it's an abrupt "No thank you I'm not interested" and on to another task. Kathy is plans ahead and anticipates how the day will unfold. She loves to read and carries a book with her during her daily excursions and reads as time and circumstances permits (e.g., while having her hair styled at the beauty salon or waiting in the doctor's office for her appointment).

She is a generous person and gives many gifts and remembers special occasions with cards; she has a list of special occasions and relationships that have to be honored. She buys, files and inventories special occasion cards for future use and will buy that "perfect gift" for someone way in advance of the occasion.

We all should be aware of the importance of regular exercise and good nutrition in our lives. A third, not as well known requirement for healthy living is proper breathing. Kathy energizes herself by taking deep breaths throughout the day. Yoga and other forms of meditation affirm the importance of deep breathing exercises.

Kathy honors her commitment to excellence by being a selective and discriminating book reader and moviegoer. She checks book and movie reviews and isn't seduced by the commercial hype that often convinces us to participate in activities that don't live up to their billing.

When you are modeling someone's behavior, the more you observe the better you emulate. I'm will never be as disciplined as Kathy, but my detailed observation of her daily living patterns has given me excellent insights and new strategies for living a fuller, more productive life.

Accelerated learning by modeling can be applied to any process that you wish to improve: negotiating skills, healthy life-style practices, weight management, risk taking, social skills, learning and planning skills, money management skills, etc.

In my *Dare To Date* class, I encourage students to closely observe and model the behavior of those with good social skills and success with the opposite sex. This was a list of observable behaviors that I compiled for people who want better success in dating:

How do they dress?
How do they greet strangers?
What is their vocabulary when talking to strangers and the opposite sex?
When and how do they smile?
What is their body language? (If you don't look approachable, you won't be approached).
How do they handle criticism?
Where do they approach the opposite sex?
What does their voice sound like?
How do they walk?

What does their posture tell you?

When I talk to groups in business settings, I always
stress how important it is to model success and give a couple
examples that can be practiced by everyone:

Observe how successful people dress and the image they project. Your wardrobe doesn't have to be
expensive. Pay attention to the little but critical
details (shoes shined, timely hair cut, clean fingernails, etc.)

Observe how the successful person shakes hands
(firm grasp and looks you in the eye).

Watch how successful people conduct themselves
in seminars. (Often sit near the front and always
participate by asking questions.)

Modeling is a learning technique that can enhance any component of your life.

Changing Emotional States

Joy is the feeling of grinning inside.

Melba Colgrove

What do we want out of life? We want to feel good. We want to be in a positive emotional state (relaxed, happy, serene, confident, determined, calm, etc.) rather than a negative emotional state (worried, anxious, depressed, scared, angry, etc.).

If environment is everything that is external to your inner being, the true essence of power is controlling how you feel *regardless* of the environment. When I choose to practice what I know, I can feel good even when I physically feel bad. We reach a point in life (I'm there), where we experience what I call "pain de jour" (pain of the day). I know that every morning when I wake up, something is going to hurt, I just don't know what it's going to be. My body has a whole bunch of choices. Regardless of the physical ailment that chooses to celebrate its existence and have its day, I always have the choice to be in good spirits and emotionally up. This requires conscious living and focusing on the good aspects of life. Sometimes pain is unavoidable, but suffering is optional. Happiness is an inside job and we can choose to avoid needless suffering. My favorite example is Helen Keller, who was deaf, dumb and blind (that certainly puts my mildly arthritic elbow into proper perspective) and yet she led a very full, joyous life and was a genuinely happy person.

I have read several biographies of people who were paralyzed and confined to a wheel chair. After they recovered from their initial period of rage and anger about the unfairness of it all, they discovered it wasn't as devastating to their happiness as we might imagine. The autobiography *Moving Violations* by John Hockenberry would be a must read, in my mind, for anyone who suddenly found themselves wheel chair bound for the rest of their life.

If happiness *wasn't* an inside job and depended upon external circumstances, how can we explain the serenity often achieved by the terminally ill? If wealth, fame and outward success were all that mattered, how do we explain the suicides of those that we thought had it made (e.g., Marilyn Monroe, Kurt Cobain, Ernest Hemingway)?

We have the power to choose how we feel. Many things that people do are poor strategies for feeling good. Excessive drinking and the use of drugs might make us feel good temporarily, but there are unwanted and undesired consequences. If you don't know how to feel good, you are probably not going to feel good. It's a skill that can be learned and has to be practiced.

An excellent exercise to expand your awareness about what makes you feel good is the development and maintenance of a " happy list." Begin compiling a list of all those things and experiences that make you feel good. This list is part of my "portable therapist kit" that I carry in my wallet. Here is an excerpt from my happy list:

> Counting my blessings
> Happy marriage
> Good health

Three wonderful kids
Unlimited possibilities for the future
Reading
Personal growth
Watching McNeil Lehrer news hour
Attending Kathy's talks and meeting new people
Anticipating future fun things
  Vacation in Florence
  Annual men's retreat
  Reestablishing contact with old friends and places
    (Arlington, Virginia & North Augusta, South
    Carolina)
Seeing "The Creation" at the Vatican
Gaining expertise in Object Oriented Technology
Tuesday night men's group
Making new friends
Intimacy
Witnessing personal growth (mine and others)
Walking
  Northtown shopping center
  Coon Rapids dam
  Nature Center
  Bicycle path
Personal ad writing
Masterpiece theater
English TV/movies
Hot luxurious showers
Riding in my car
Outside on nice days
Talking to my kids
Creating a new idea
Remembering a wonderful experience
  Phone call from Holly
  Glen Leet's lunch with Margaret Mead
  John Kennedy's comments on system
Learning something new

Listening to music
Watching boxing
Watching basketball
Watching football
Flowers
Bookstore browsing
Flower Shop browsing
Buying books
Getting a bargain
Farmer's market
Travel
People watching
New Yorker cartoons
Sunday paper
Winning Way newsletter
Oprah
Mail
Telephone messages
Pet store browsing
Onions in Gibsons
Smile from a pretty girl
Innocence and joy of children
Kathy (love of my life)
Kathy's relatives
Kimber
Duane
Greg
Riley Jr.
Randy
Sean
Our apartment after Karen's cleans
Humor
Irony
Computer technology
Creative business cards
Yellow legal pads

Yellow pencils with erasers that erase
Updating happy list
Living in Minnesota
    (Friendly people, beautiful scenery, birds)
Attending first rate plays and musicals
Going to a play and having the best seats in the house
Sleeping in a king size bed
Glycerin soap
Scented candles
Peaches (my longhaired tri-colored cat)
Finding Subway stamps
Free cafe mocha at Borders bookstore
Reading in sunlit warmth at Borders book store
When I truly understand that I always have
    freedom and choice

The happy list makes you focus on what's enjoyable in your life. I use this exercise in workshops and discovered that people who can make the longest lists seem to be the happier than those that struggle with the exercise. Gratitude can be learned and the happiest people are the most grateful people.

Happiness is a learned skill. If you don't know what makes you happy, how can you pursue it or experience gratitude for the many wonderful things in your life? When you are suffering from the blahs or having a blue Monday, the happy list can lift your spirits. Read the list carefully, slowly *savoring* each experience listed and your mood will change. If you are really down, read the list multiple times until you feel better. It is effective for changing emotional states

We want to continually develop awareness about what puts us into a positive emotional state. What makes you feel good doesn't necessarily have to be logical and make sense. If you work for a large organization and receive an annual pay raise, it might not make you feel good. You might consider it as part of the job, an entitlement for working within a large organization. Contrast that feeling with the feeling you would experience when finding a twenty-dollar bill while walking to lunch. That chance happening might create much more excitement and good feeling than the routine salary raise which represents substantially more money.

I often eat Subway sandwiches for lunch. Each time you buy a sandwich, you are given stamps that you paste onto a little coupon card, and when the card is filled, you are entitled to a free sandwich. One of the highlights of my day is when I find a subway stamp on the floor or on the counter left behind by a previous customer. One day I found six stamps and you would have thought I won the lottery. I was over the moon.

Finding a great parking spot provides my wife a joy that quite honestly I don't fully understand. Maybe it's a gender thing.

It's not important for the things that bring us joy to make sense, but it is important for us to know what does bring us joy. Nothing but good can come from this awareness. There are movie scenes that I can recall which will always make me laugh and bring a smile to my face. Build your own little virtual library of favorite movie moments that when recalled makes you happy. The point is that we have control over how we feel. We can change our emotional states.

You will discover that you can create specific emotional states for specific purposes.

When I would go for a job interview, I would find it important to go from a casual informal state to a more professional state. I would get a haircut, shine my shoes and have my suit pressed and carry my briefcase. It transforms me into more of a professional person. My demeanor became much more serious, my confidence increases, my body language changes and my language/vocabulary became more consistent with that of the business world.

When dating after my first divorce, I discovered techniques that would allow me to enter a "social/charming" state. For first dates, I would always wear something that I really felt good in and that was consistent with who I really was (Harris Tweeds yes, business suits no). I would also choose a setting (a favorite restaurant) that had the ambiance that I desired and that I would be comfortable in. Meeting someone for a quick lunch at noon never worked for me and would not provide an atmosphere that would allow me to put my best foot forward socially.

If I am trying something new, my strategy for putting myself into a state of confidence would be to put myself in touch with prior successes that were related and supportive of my new venture (e.g. when I had taken a risk and had achieved success). I would visualize and relive those successes. I would review what I know about handling fear and would make it my ally rather than considering it the enemy. When I begun doing seminars and three hour lectures, I would relive all the positive experiences I had when I was a member of Toastmasters and replay in my mind all the supportive, nurturing feedback received.

When I write, I want to be in a creative state. I pay close attention to what creates an environment that stimulates my creativity. Understanding the connection between a high-energy state and creativity, I coordinate my creative activities with my high-energy phases. I know what rituals are necessary to induce creativity for me. I know what components of my environment enhance or detract from my creativity - what types of background music are optimum, what type of lighting, how much exposure and interaction with other people is permissible, etc.

With awareness we can learn to manage our emotional states.

Who Are You?

If anything is to happen, it has to start with us,
individually, in our own place and time. To
wait for a leader to guide us into the future is to
be forever disillusioned.

Charles Handy

We often become defined by happenstance and default.
Our career, important relationships and lifestyle just happen.
We follow the path of least resistance, do what we comfortably know, repeat the same learned behaviors, travel the
same path and accept the same disempowering and limiting
beliefs. We are reluctant to engage in a serious process of
self-discovery and are fearful of being authentic. We all need
to continually work on discovering and honoring our core
essence. It isn't a one-time event; we change and circumstances change. It needs to be an ongoing pursuit of determining who you are, what you want and developing the
courage to be that person.

The times in my life that I've really gotten myself in
trouble and led a joyless, meaningless, shallow existence was
when I was pretending to be other than who I really was.

Doing work that is consistent with who you are is absolutely essential if you want to feel fulfilled by living a purposeful and meaningful existence. Life without purpose
doesn't work. You will go through life coping rather than

rejoicing. Whenever someone in counseling tells me that they are bored, I know the problem: lack of purpose. Boredom is often perched on the top of a very slippery slope that can lead to ennui, despair, mild depression and then deeper depression.

Taking Responsibility For One's Actions

It is no use walking anywhere to preach unless our walking is our preaching.

St. Francis of Assisi

People in counseling often begin with the mindset that the counselor is the expert and will fix them with minimal effort on their part. The reality is that the counselor or coach is merely a catalyst of change. The client has to do the heavy lifting. If you aren't willing to do the work, the probability of meaningful and lasting change is remote. You can never be truly happy by evading or abdicating responsibility for your life.

Some people misunderstand responsibility to be blame. They blame circumstances (My genes/upbringing/astrological chart is responsible!) or others (The Devil made me do it! My parents/spouse/boss are responsible!) or they blame themselves (It's my fault. I'll emotionally flagellate myself.) This concept of "responsibility" doesn't admit any real possibility to change. Blame is disempowering. The test of "taking responsibility" is whether you are empowering yourself as able to do something about it. We have the power to understand the consequences of different actions and power of choice over what actions to take. By consistently accepting that we do choose and accepting the consequences of our choices, we can increase our understanding and ability to decide.

Nathaniel Branden in his book *Honoring The Self* examines the value of taking responsibility for one's actions *in the moment of performing the action.* He gives the following examples:

Right now I am choosing not to do the work I promised my boss I would do, and I plan to alibi later - and I take responsibility for that.

Right now I am choosing not to answer, honestly and directly, my wife's question - and I take responsibility for that.

Right now I am choosing not to deal with the look of pain in my child's eyes- and I take responsibility for that.

Right now I am choosing to steal this money from my guest's handbag- and I take responsibility for that.

Right now I am choosing to stay home and feel sorry for myself rather than go out and look for a job- and I take responsibility for that.

Right now I am choosing to procrastinate rather than confront an issue with my friend/spouse/employee/employer/colleague that I know needs to be confronted -and I take responsibility for that.

Right now I am choosing to pretend that I am indifferent when the truth is I am hurting- and I take responsibility for that.

Right now I am choosing to act tough when the truth is

I want to reach out for help- and I take responsibility for that.

This is powerful self-talk. It would be extremely difficulty to have this type of dialogue with one's self and not see the potential damage that one's self-esteem would suffer by not taking personal responsibility. This type of self-talk forces us to see the negative consequences when we aren't willing to take responsibility. When we aren't willing to reflect on our actions and behavior *while they are happening*, it's a form of denial or avoidance. When we habitualize avoidance of truth, it becomes a denial of life and a denial of the power of choice. That's the worst form of being stuck. You and you alone have to take responsibility. A victim's mentality believes you should rely on others more than yourself. It creates an unhealthy state of dependency. You must make your own decisions and live your own life. Assume nobody is going to come to the rescue. Your therapist will listen; he is paid to. Your doctor will write you a prescription; he is highly paid to. Your wife and your friends will listen and cluck their tongues in sympathy. But the unvarnished reality is that they have their own problems and agendas and their problems are always going to have priority over your problems. I honestly believe that writers of self help books and therapists do it as much for themselves as they do it for clients and others. We all need to be heard; we all crave recognition.

When I thought I had prostrate cancer, my wife and friends were sympathetic. However, nobody really cared like I did. Why? Because it was my problem and not theirs. How did I know it's my problem? Because I am the one who will have to suffer the consequences. The doctor will see me dispassionately and determines the course of treatment based on probabilities and treats me accordingly. It's really not his problem.

Once I took ownership of the problem, I begun to be

proactive and examined my options and selected the best option available to me rather than saying "Well, the doctors in my health care system know best," or "What do I know? They are the experts." I know that I am truly responsible for my health and I must have the courage to question, examine and select the best options for me. We must take responsibility for all aspects of our lives.

Don't Tell Me You Aren't Highly Creative

The greatest goal in life is not the attainment of fame. The principle thing in this world is to keep one's soul aloft.

Gustave Flaubert

We are all creative geniuses. As children we are spontaneous, highly imaginative and creative. Children sometimes have "make believe" friends. Kids don't need expensive toys; they know that a plain cardboard box is really a castle. They understand some minor remodeling might be required such as creating windows by punching holes in the box. All kids know that a good castle requires windows.

When I was a kid growing up in South Carolina, nobody ever bought me a kite. Flying things in the air is fun, so I had to improvise. I used to catch large June bugs and bumble bees, attach thread to them and "fly" them. In retrospect, I think it was a breakthrough in kite technology; I never had to wait for a windy day.

As we grow up, we lose our innocence, spontaneity and creativity. We cease to trust our instincts as to what will bring us joy. We begin to march to the beat of other peoples' drums. We no longer do what is right for us; we become warped by societal expectations, misguided parental guidance and other external influences. Over the years, we begin to forget who we really are and lose touch with what brings us happiness and joy. Our creativity becomes buried and suppressed. It's no longer reflected in our work or daily living. You need to know that it's still there. You are still a creative genius. The question is how to get in touch with your creativity. Some us of just have to dig a little deeper than others do to find it.

We often define creativity too narrowly, thinking of it as being the exclusive domain of the artist, writer, painter, sculptor, etc. Creativity can manifest itself in all walks of life by a whole variety of people engaged in all kinds of activities. To me, creativity is just growing and realizing more of your untapped potential in a way that makes your life work better. It could be problem solving at work, creating more intimacy in relationships, better parenting solutions or other ways to make your life or job more fun and joyful.

Creativity is a mindset, a skill that can permeate all areas of your life.

We underestimate the power of creativity to enhance and improve our lives. If you nurture creativity in one part of your life, you'll soon discover that creativity begins to flourish in other areas of your life. Studies show that creative people possess many positive qualities:

Getting along better with others
Better planning and problem resolution skills
Greater enjoyment of life
Seeing and understanding better the big picture

All our lives we have been gathering information through our 5 senses and storing the memories. Think of your mind as a huge data bank with all this data carefully filed. The conscious mind has access to about 1% of this mental database and the subconscious has access to the rest. If we can learn ways to access all the data we possess (e.g., questioning the status quo, brainstorming, certain forms of meditation, the use of affirmations, communing with nature, stream of consciousness journaling techniques, visualization exercises, etc.), our creativity will soar. Creative people have more faith and trust in their gut instincts, hunches and intuition. They knowingly or unknowingly use strategies that routinely access all parts of their mind.

Demystifying Creativity

What lies behind us and what lies before us are tiny matters, compared to what lies within us.

Emerson

Creativity can be induced and frustration can be minimized, if you understand the natural flow and dynamics of the steps within the creative process:

Preparation - This is the data gathering phase. You collect all the information, do the research and analysis.

Yet when you are done, the answer to your problem or dilemma often will not immediately come forth. You feel stymied, frustrated and stumped. This is when you need to walk away from the problem; take a break and do something different.

Incubation - All the raw material and information gathered in the preparation phase begins to percolate on an unconscious level and insights begin slowly to seep into your consciousness. It's a critical phase, which involves letting go of the problem (consciously or unconsciously), putting it on the back burner and letting your subconscious chew on it for awhile. When you have studied a problem and you say to yourself, "I'll sleep on it," that's the correct strategy. Allow your subconscious to take over and process the data you have collected in your conscious state.

Illumination - This is the "AHA!" stage in achieving breakthrough insights. You never know when it's going to occur. Albert Einstein said, "Why is it, I always get my best ideas while shaving?" Remember the Boy Scout motto - always be prepared. Be prepared at all times to catch ideas. There is no way to predict exactly when a great idea is likely to pop into your mind. Some of my best thoughts have occurred in the most unlikely place or at the most inconvenient time:

Dreams can be a great source for insights and creativity; I keep a pencil and paper on my nightstand to capture those middle of the night ideas.

The shower, bathing, brushing teeth, the toilet: creativity knows no boundaries and doesn't punch a time clock.

In the kitchen while cooking, commuting, out to lunch (both interpretations are valid - eating or daydreaming), at a coffee shop, playing sports or working out at the gym.

Ideas are thoughts and thoughts are ephemeral. Unless you make the effort to capture your ideas, you will lose many of them. If you are serious about not letting your good ideas escape, carry a recording medium with you at all times. A starting point would be a pencil and paper. You could also use 3x5 index cards (they are easier to sort and categorize). After having a near miss while driving, I learned that it's not always convenient to take written notes. I decided to augment my basic system of note taking. I purchased a little micro-cassette-recording device that's much smaller than a pack of cigarettes and has a chip that can record up to 5 minutes of dictation or conversation. This makes for safer driving.

I have heard of creative people that have a device that allows them to jot down their thoughts while taking showers.

My wife and I purchased some software from 3M that allows you to paste "Post It Notes" on the computer monitor. This is real handy when you are in the middle of a computer session and you think of something you need to write down or the phone rings and it's a message for your spouse. The post it note reduces the risk of the message being lost (it's also legible; sometimes I've hastily jotted down a phone message which was indecipherable even to me). Kathy and I always know where to find our phone messages.

Kathy also mails herself emails from work to home as reminder notices for things requiring further attention. If you have a cell phone, you can leave messages on your voice mail system or answering machine.

When you become rich and famous, you can hire a personal assistant who follows you around recording all the profound and creative things you are thinking. If you haven't achieved that level of success, maybe you can con your spouse or one of your kids to play the role of dutiful assistant. (I shudder to think what would happen if I made that suggestion to my wife.) The point is to be prepared at all times to catch ideas.

Once you have established the habit of carrying idea-catching material, you will be surprised at what your mind produces and how creative you are.

A final word on the illumination phase. Have you ever had an insight or creative idea while driving to work and said to yourself "I'll follow up on this tonight when I have more time"? Evening comes and you discover that you can't recreate or connect meaningfully with what you were previously thinking about. Emerson said, "Look sharply after our thoughts. They come, unlooked for, like a new bird in your trees and if you turn to your usual task, disappear." Sudden flashes of inspiration or insights have a vividness and certainty, that is lost if you try to recreate or reconstruct the moment at a later time. This is why it's essential to capture the thought in its original and most creative form.

Verification - This is the last phase and simply involves trying out the solution to make sure it works.

When you understand the 4 steps of the creative process, you become more attuned to and find it easier to go with the creative flow. It also gives you confidence not to panic or become overwhelmed when you are stuck in the data-gathering phase.

Capturing Creativity And
Keeping It

**Experience teaches us in a millennium
what passion teaches us in an hour.**

Ralph Iron

After you train yourself to capture all those creative thoughts, the next step is the storage and filing. One of my sons is terribly creative and always carries pencils, sketchpads and writing paper. He records oodles of brilliant and creative thoughts - futuristic concepts that are just beyond the cutting edge of technology. The only problem is he loses them!

You need some type of basic repository or an elementary filing system. A start can be an idea bank where you deposit all your notes, cocktail napkin doodles, etc. The idea bank could be as rudimentary as a file folder, empty desk drawer, shoebox or a card index file. Computers have great data base systems that can be used for information storage and retrieval purposes.

A word of caution for novice computer users: always back up your files with a second copy (hard copy, floppy disk, zip drive etc.). Hard drives can crash or be eaten by viruses. Further precautions can be taken, if you truly value your intellectual property and you are engaged in some large creative endeavor such as writing a book. You might sleep better at night if you developed the habit of routinely storing a back-up copy off site. Kathryn Bates and Elizabeth Ross Kubler (both writers) lost years of research and notes when their houses burned down. I make back up copies of all my work every 3 months and store it at a friend's house. Furniture and clothes can be replaced; research notes, class materials and current writing projects would be much harder.

For me, writing is both a means and an end. The act of writing and note taking are both therapeutic and a necessary part of my daily life. I love the act of writing and the feeling of accomplishment when articles and books are published.

The more research and writing you do, the more interested you will become learning better, more creative and efficient note-taking techniques. I'm always trying to lessen the drudgery and make the recall and retrieval process easier. I bought a lap top computer thinking that instead of writing notes in long hand and later entering them into the computer, I could combine two steps into one and type instead of write. I discovered that typing inhibits my creativity. I focus more on the process (OOPS, I hit the caps lock key and now I have to backspace to the beginning of the line and start all over) rather than the essence of what I'm writing. When I just let it rip, flow and spew out in my barely legible writing, trusting that I'll by able to interpret and decipher at data entry time, I seem to establish a direct line to my creativity. *The Artist's Way* by Julia Cameron is an unequivocal must read, if you are serious about unlocking your creativity. She makes this same point. She recommends that you do your "Morning Pages" in long hand (3 pages of daily journaling). The real value and joy that my lap top computer provides is portability. I can do my data entry wherever I choose - Barnes and Noble bookstore, any comfortable chair at home or my favorite local coffee cafe.

Here are some note-taking tricks that might work for you:

Next time you go to a seminar or workshop, try this strategy. Establish different categories. For each category, write its name on the top of a different sheet of paper. This will help you decide what type of information you are interested in collecting and will ensure that it will be better organized afterwards. It's OK to have a misc. category for all that data that you discovered you needed and didn't plan for.

Check out a concept called Mindmapping. (If you have a background in data processing you might remember a similar process called entity diagramming.) Mindmapping incorporates the use of symbols in note taking and allows you to place all logical and relevant information together. It's easier to define complex relationship with symbols and connecting lines rather than the exclusive use of text or narrative. If you were interviewing a busy executive with limited availability and were trying to understand the organizational structure of his company or his department, you would be able to grasp complex relationships involving ideas and people faster and easier. It also facilitates the process of adding and documenting new relationships. Written narrative operates more on a first come first written down structure and evolves into a less logical structure. If you want more information, refer to *The Mind Map Book* by Tony Buzan.

Here is a technique that really works for me. I visualize the blank page as having 5 different sections (top, bottom, right margin, left margin and the center). The center is the core and where I place the majority of my notes. I designate the other sections for specialized note-taking requirements or reminder areas. I use the left margin to record other books and authors that I might want to investigate further.

The right margin I use to jot down inspirational sayings that I might wish to use in a book or article. The top section is used to list tasks that need to be done ASAP. The bottom is used to jot down notes that are out of context or flow with what I'm writing in the center section. This technique allows me to easily locate sayings, book titles and other specialty data without having to pore through all my notes. It's a real time saver for me.

Another variation of the practice is to color code what you write. Maybe red could be used to convey a sense of urgency and blue for topics related to long range planning, or projects with no deadline established. If this appeals to you, buy yourself a 4-color pen and experiment with it. If it doesn't work out, you still have an unusual pen for only a couple of bucks.

You Are Smarter
Than You Think

Everyone has been made for some particular
work and the desire for that work has been put
in his or her heart.

Rumi

Howard Gardener, a Harvard psychologist, believes
there are multiple types of intelligence. Our school experiences have led us to believe that those who do well on IQ
tests or have achieved high SAT scores are the smart ones
and the rest of us are average or worse. The damage done by
defining intelligence in a too narrow context is that it affects
our self-esteem and becomes a self-fulfilling prophecy. If
you believe you are average, you will act accordingly. You
can never outperform your self-image.

There is a classic experiment in which a group of kids
were told that those among them who had blue eyes were
smarter and those that had brown eyes were mentally infe-
rior. The kids' performances were consistent with how they
had been labeled.

There is an obvious bias in favor of those who do well
on intelligence tests. They are considered smart, receive
preferential treatment (sometimes not knowingly) and have a
better shot at the more prestigious schools. Those who
received lower SAT scores are labeled as average or damaged

goods and labor under the illusion that they have nothing going for them, because their skills, intelligence and potential haven't been properly identified. Acing SAT tests just might just say that you good at taking tests and nothing more; some people are good at taking tests. Of course, it may also say other things and I don't mean to imply that scoring high on these types of test is without merit, but it isn't that strong of predictor as to how successful you will be in life. There are many underachievers and unhappy people who do well on tests and fare poorly in life. Let's review the seven types of intelligences identified by Howard Gardener:

Linguistic intelligence is the intelligence of words. This is the intelligence of successful writers, storytellers and poets. People who are particularly smart in this area can argue, persuade, entertain, teach or instruct. These are the people we call wordsmiths.

Logical/mathematical intelligence relates to numbers and logic. This is the intelligence of the mathematician, accountant and computer programmer.

Spatial intelligent is the third kind of smarts. It involves thinking in pictures and images. It's the domain of architects, photographers and artists.

Musical intelligence is the fourth kind of smarts. People blessed with this have the capacity to perceive, appreciate and produce rhythms and melodies.

Bodily/Kinetics intelligence refers to the physical self. It includes talent in controlling one's body movements and also in handling objects skillfully. Good hand eye coordination is an example. Athletes, artisans, mechanics and surgeons possess a great measure of this kind of intelligence.

Interpersonal is the ability to understand and work with other people. It involves being able to perceive and be responsive to the moods, temperament and desires of others. An example might be a social coordinator for a singles club.

Intrapersonal is the intelligence of the inner self. Counselors and therapists have good intrapersonal skills. They can be very introspective, contemplative and enjoy various forms of soul searching.

You might strongly identify with one or two of the above descriptions, but you actually possess all 7 types of intelligence.

When these intelligences get way out of balance and one is highly developed at the expense of all the others, we get idiot savants like Raymond in the movie Rainmaker who could calculate numbers with lightening speed but couldn't take care of himself.

The important thing to remember is that you should give all these intelligences equal billing when evaluating how smart you are. Book smarts get all the press, but I know many successful people whose street smarts more than compensate for any alleged lack of book smarts or formal education.

There are lessons to be learned from highly creative and extraordinary individuals. Highly accomplished individuals are able to identify their strengths and then follow a path that utilizes and exploits their talents. You don't want to become an unhappy doctor or lawyer just because your father wanted you to follow in his footsteps when you were really meant to be a musician. It's a prescription for frustration rather than happiness.

Oprah Winfrey has incredible talent in front of a camera or live audience, but she would be the first to tell you that there are innumerable talents and abilities she sees in her various guests each week that she herself does not possess.

Bill Gates said Microsoft would be only a fraction of what it is today if it wasn't for the talents and abilities of his partners.

Steven Scott said that he only has four significant talents: he knows how to type reasonably well, he knows how to effectively and persuasively communicate, he knows how to direct on-camera talents and he knows how to market products and ideas. He can't play a musical instrument. He doesn't understand accounting or computers, possesses no mechanical skills and yet he has generated over one billion in sales and created multiple companies from insurance to cosmetics.

The lesson these examples can teach us is you have to identify your strengths (intelligences) and focus on them.

Is That Cup Half Full
Or Half Empty?

**Gratitude unlocks the fullness of life. It turns
what we have into enough, and more. It turns
denial into acceptance, chaos to order, confu-
sion to clarity. It can turn a meal into a feast, a
house into a home, a stranger into a friend.
Gratitude makes sense of our past, brings
peace for today, and creates a vision for tomorrow.**

Melody Beattie

A strategy that is second nature to people who live life
effectively is the use of paradigm shifts. It's also called
reframing or altered perception. Mary Ann Williamson in
Return To Love defines a miracle as a change in perception.
Sometimes we can't change a situation or circumstance, but
we can change how we view and perceive it. Always question
the challenges in life by asking, "Is there a better interpretation? Is there a way that I can look at this that's good for me
rather than bad?" It's a strategy that helps you be a more
positive thinking person and see possibilities rather than
limitations.

My favorite example of a paradigm shift occurred in
Milwaukee at that city's best German restaurant. The joint
was jumping and the waitresses had to hustle to keep up. We
had ordered desert and when mine arrived, it wasn't what I
anticipated and I asked the waitress if I could change my
dessert order. She said with a big smile, "No problem," and
I almost felt that I was doing her a favor. This really puzzled
me because I knew how busy she was and that the waitresses

were responsible for making the deserts. Most waitresses would be annoyed and resentful at a customer changing his mind at the last moment and creating additional work during their rush period.

When we were served our coffee, I asked why she wasn't upset when I requested a different desert. She smiled again and said, "All the busboys that work here are over-worked and underpaid. Whenever there is a mistake on a desert order, I get to give it to one of the busboys and that makes me feel good." She had found a way to feel good about a problem that would be very upsetting to most waitresses.

I used to drive a 1984 Honda Prelude. I had two ways to view my ownership of an old car. I was driving a rusted out junker or I was the proud owner of an unrestored classic.

When Kathy and I started dating, we inadvertently walked through some wet cement and left footprints. Kathy was concerned that we were going to get into trouble. I said in my terribly witty and sometimes obnoxious way "Don't worry. They will be looking for two men." Kathy is a big gal and wears size 10 shoes. Instead of being shamed and becoming indignant, she chose to see the humor in the situation and laughed heartily. Kathy gives presentations to groups of large size women on body image issues. She tells this story comfortably and never fails to get a laugh.

Kathy not only has a large physical presence, but also projects a "larger than life" image with her high energy, desire to do everything quickly and passionate zest for living life fully. She is an Ethel Merman type who frequently bursts into song, singing some Broadway show tune that she has lovingly committed to memory. When I get up in the morning, I love my quiet time and solitude. When Kathy gets up she is doing all those noisy, necessary things (blow drying her hair, doing a load of laundry or starting up the dish washer) that need to be done before she is off to work. This used to irritate me even though I knew it was temporary and

I would get my solitude once she left for work. Now when I was a kid, I owned a St. Bernard dog. It was the most impractical pet imaginable for a family living in suburbia in a small house with a tiny yard. Bernie would howl at nighttime and leave the house in shambles with overturned furniture, broken vases and scratched up wallpaper. I loved that dog so much that his "minor shortcomings" just didn't matter to me. (Mom and dad saw it slightly differently.) Whenever Kathy is noisily clunking around the house in the morning, I think of Bernie and realize that I love Kathy so much that it really doesn't matter. It's a small, small problem in the big, big scheme of things. We can learn to view things differently and in a way that makes us feel good rather than bad.

Positive Thinking

Attention is the key; for where man's attention goes, there goes his energy and he himself can only follow.

Saint Germain

I suspect that positive thinking isn't properly appreciated because people aren't aware of the specific, tangible benefits that flow from positive thinking. Many mistakenly believe that positive thinking only creates fuzzy feelings of well being and not much else. They will concede that these feelings might be nice but in the real world we need no-nonsense strategies that provide concrete, specific, measurable results. If you pooh-pooh positive thinking, consider the following:

Positive thinkers have a higher level of energy. This allows them to lead a fuller life and accomplish more, which makes them feel good. This reinforces their optimistic view of life

Positive thinking leads to a healthier life. Many books and studies have documented the mind/body connection and the harmful impact that negative thinking and stress can have on your immune system.

There is a greater likelihood that good things will happen to you when you are in positive frame of mind. Most good action and sensible risk-taking occurs when you are in a positive mood. Negative thinking reduces the possibility of action, because you are focused on the possible negative consequences and are blinded to the possibilities of life

Like attracts like. Positive thinking, upbeat, confident people attract similar people into their lives. They attract the kind of people whose motto for living is "Let's do it" or "Let's make it happen" or "Let's take a chance; let's do something new and different" or "Let's have fun." Negative people attract those who feel more comfortable saying, "That will never work," or "You better not take a chance," or "We are not good enough to do that," or "What will other people think? We better play it safe."

Pessimists create unnecessary suffering. Optimists maximize the joy of living.

Moments To Remember

Have you really lived ten thousand or more days, or have you lived one day ten thousand or more times?

Wayne Dyer

One of my favorite quotes is by a trapeze artist after he suffered a terrible accident in which he was severely hurt and several members of his family were killed. After a long and painful recuperation, he returned to work and begun perfecting a high-risk, "death defying" trapeze act. He was asked why, after such a terrible accident, he was back performing again. He said "These are the moments I'm alive; all else is waiting." That's the essence of fond memories, those moments in which we feel fully alive. To experience life fully and to have these moments, we must be willing to take risks and step out of our comfort zone. We must do what initially feels terribly uncomfortable and also must accept that there are no guarantees in life. Balloons break, love affairs end and everybody has to visit the dentist.

If we aren't willing to change our living patterns, we consign ourselves to a sameness that creates boredom and ennui. You will have discovered the perfect formula for being perpetually restless and discontent. These moments of feeling alive are the moments I live for. These are those moments of ecstasy, passion and appreciation of beauty. These are the moments that fill me with gratitude and inspire me to be my best. For in these moments, I know that this is the answer to my search for meaning and purpose in life.

Kathy and I recently spent 10 days in Rome and had experiences that I will treasure for the rest of my life. One evening we were stumbling around like lost, bewildered tourists looking for a particular restaurant and having no luck. We turned the corner and there was the Pantheon, lit up with floodlights, a 2,000 year old building of indescribable beauty. It literally took my breath away.

A few days later, we went to the Vatican and saw Michelangelo's Sistine Chapel. Another "once in a lifetime," awe inspiring and humbling moment. Experiencing the wonder, beauty and genius of Michelangelo set the stage for another one of those "moments." On our first day in Rome, we had met and befriended a young lady from Greece. A few days later we bumped into her in front of our hotel and invited her to check out our accommodations (she was a tour guide and wanted to know more about our hotel). While in the room, we begun to talk about the wonderful sites in Rome and how we were all deeply moved by the beauty of the Sistine Chapel. Kathy begun to read some quotes and comments about Michelangelo, the Sistine Chapel and Pope Julius the 2nd, who commissioned the work.

Michelangelo wasn't keen on painting the chapel ceiling; he wanted to sculpture. Reluctance is an understatement; Michelangelo characterized one of his meetings with the Pope by saying, "I was forced to go with a halter round my neck".

The next passage is from a letter of introduction introducing Michelangelo to the Pope and gives insight into how the pope managed to get Michelangelo to undertake this Herculean task:

"The bearer of these presents will be

Michelangelo the sculptor, whom we send to please and satisfy His Holiness. We certify that he is an excellent young man, and in his own art without peer in Italy, perhaps even in the universe. His nature is such that he requires to be drawn out by kindness and encouragement; but, if love is shown him and he is well treated, he will accomplish things which will make the whole world wonder."

Centuries later another genius, Goethe, said that no one who has not seen the Sistine Chapel can have a complete conception of what a single man can accomplish.

All three of us were choked up by these passages that helped explain so accurately our feelings and some of the history that lead to the creation of this divine masterpiece. Anna had been a virtual stranger to us and yet in that moment we felt deeply connected. These moments of aliveness and feeling connected were worth whatever price had to be paid in terms of lack of comfort and the awkwardness of being an American in a foreign country and a different culture. We are already planning our next venture abroad. Paris! Here we come.

Cultivating Awareness

Perhaps if one really knew when one was
happy one would know the things that were
necessary for one's life.

Joanna Field

Over time we can become a series of conditioned
responses and our spontaneity and awareness is greatly
diminished. Up to 95% of the average person's behavior is
nothing more than conditioned responses. We become creatures of habit in both our thinking and our behavior. The
average person has 40,000 to 60,000 thoughts daily. Unfortunately 90% of the thoughts you have today have been
recycled from the previous day. We get into the habit of
thinking the same thoughts day in and day out. Habits rule
our lives. Habits help explain why people continue to work
at the same job, associate with the same people, drive the
same route to work, engage in the same leisure activities,
watch the same TV shows and read the same type of books.

To help you better understand what I mean by conditioned responses, imagine the following scenario:

At a crowded restaurant a woman
screams; stands up, slaps the face of her date
and storms out of the restaurant. The reac-

tions among the people in the restaurant vary. One man is terribly upset; a young teenager is angry; a divorcee is saddened; a counselor is curious; a pastor is embarrassed; the waiter is amused and another couple ignores the whole scene.

The same event triggered a different response in each of the observers.

Our response is determined by how we have been conditioned by prior life experiences. It is often an automatic, knee jerk type of feeling and reaction. The man who was terribly upset painfully remembers being struck by his mom as a child. The teenager thinks this is just another example that women can get away with anything (just like his sister never gets yelled at and his mom and dad are always screaming at him). The divorcee sees it as yet another example of the conflict between men and women. The counselor is curious about the dynamics of the relationship that resulted in the woman's angry response. The pastor is shamed by the possibility that these people are in his congregation and are setting a bad example for others. The waiter has seen it all and is no longer surprised or upset by people's behavior, especially after they have had a couple of drinks. The couple have become sophisticated and jaded; they feign indifference.

Most of what we think, feel and the way we respond is based on prior conditioning. Greater awareness allows you more choices. Without choices, change is not possible. Awareness is a skill that can be learned and practiced. You can begin to examine patterns of behavior and habits and assess whether they are desirable or unwanted. Good habits (e.g. brushing your teeth twice a day) don't need to be addressed; other habits need to be brought to the light of day and modified or eliminated. A lot of automatic behavior is benign and heightened awareness of this kind of behavior doesn't provide opportunities for significant change and personal growth. Men get into the habit of always first putting on either their shirts or their pants when dressing. Men who shave start shaving in the same spot each time. There isn't much payback in terms of personal growth to modify this type of behavior. It's only important to grasp how much of our behavior is automatic. We sleep on the same side of the bed each night. If you want to understand the power of a habit, try convincing your significant other to swap sides of the bed. It ain't going to happen.

When we living unconsciously, we aren't living in the present. We aren't responding to what is currently happening. Our lives are being conditioned and controlled by the past. When we are chained to the past, our choices are limited.

Have you every encountered a total stranger and felt an instant like or dislike? You are projecting attributes of someone from your past onto this person. Perhaps a former boss, a controlling father or an ex boyfriend.

Lack of awareness condemns you to going through life on automatic pilot, repeating the same patterns of behavior that create the same predictable results. One definition of insanity is doing the same things over and over and expecting different results.

Heightened awareness enables you to better interpret the signposts and clues strewn along the path that you are traveling and assists you in understanding what you should be doing and what decisions you need to make. We need to learn how to pay attention to these messages that are telling us who we really are and what we truly need.

All my life I have been fascinated with human potential and self-empowerment. I love to read and prefer non-fiction books that focus on some aspect of personal growth. Every book I own has been "magic markered" to death and contains scribbled notes in the margins. I take copious notes on whatever is available - yellow pads, cocktail napkins, the back of business cards; you name it and I've written on it. Imbedded in all of this behavior were clues that were telling me what my real passions were and what I should be doing with my life. If I had had the courage to pay attention and to acknowledge how important these clues were in helping me understand who I really was and what I really should be doing with my life, I would have pursued a career or calling that was in line with my real interests (writing and teaching) much earlier in life.

Heightened awareness and acceptance of the real me allowed me to acknowledge my strong introversion and need for ample personal space and solitude. If I don't have a few hours to myself everyday, my life doesn't work. I don't leave this to chance. I make sure that I get and also my wife gets the necessary amount of solitude we both need. Introverts are energized by thinking, whereas people and social contact energize extroverts. We introverts like people in small doses and prefer one-to-one relationships and meaningful conversion. We believe the larger the group, the smaller the conversation. We aren't into small talk. My first wife was much more extroverted than I and required much more social contact; she enjoyed parties and large social functions. This lack of awareness about who we were and what we needed created a perpetual disagreement as to how we should spend our time. This was a big factor in the marriage not working and ultimately ending in divorce.

One of my biggest moments of revelation was when I accepted the reality that no matter how well paid I was and how well others thought I did my job, if the work wasn't in alignment with who I really was, I didn't have a snowball's chance in hell of really being happy. I was in marketing for a small company and my boss was happy because I would always make my sales quota, the customers were satisfied because I listened and provided good customer service. Everyone was happy or reasonably satisfied, except one person and I was that person, the person whose opinion I most needed to listen to.

Marketing jobs are a good fit for extroverts, those who like to mingle and genuinely enjoy the wining, dining and schmoozing part of the job. This wasn't me; I much preferred being in my office thinking deep thoughts rather than engaging in small talk and chitchat with clients. It wasn't that I couldn't do it reasonably well, it was just that I didn't enjoy it.

This was a watershed epiphany for me. The awareness that I desperately needed to be myself and find work and a career that allowed me to use rather than suppress my natural and real desires. So I said to myself, "OK, Riley, accept that you are a flaming introvert - what now?" I would always test off the scale for introversion whenever I took a vocational aptitude test. Being a lighthouse keeper on a small desolate island off the coast of New England never sounded that bad to me. I do wonder, however, how lighthouse keepers handle the need for hazelnut-flavored coffee in the morning.

When I begun to allow the real me to surface and to develop the skills and the courage to pursue my passion and realness, my life slowly transformed from a financially well heeled, purposeless existence to an existence of having all I really needed, plus purpose that gave everyday meaning. I began to write, publishing a couple of short articles on self-help and producing a newsletter called the *Winner's Edge*. I wouldn't want to apply any type of cost accounting or profit analysis to my earlier efforts; they were labors of love. I do know that I was much happier following this path and always had enough money to enjoy life.

In the earlier stages, my wife was concerned that I was following a path to financial oblivion and ultimately would become a homeless street person. My Smart Alec response would always be "But the real question is, would I be a happy street person?" What I discovered is that when you begin going down the right path everything turns out OK, and it's a much more pleasurable journey.

Writing is natural for an introvert; it requires lots of thinking, observing (witnessing life) and solitude. I also began to do some counseling; good counseling is intense and devoid of small talk. Meaningful conversation and intelligent dialogue is what introverts crave. I began teaching and doing self-empowerment seminars. The preparation for a class or series of lectures requires research, reading, thinking, interpretation, synthesis and stitching information from multiple disparate sources into a seamless presentation that has meaning and value for the class members. All of these endeavors are consistent with who I am and provides me with a feeling of profound gratitude knowing that I'm on the right track and am living a purposeful conscious life.

Awareness means paying attention to messages you are receiving and often choose to ignore. Do you have recurring dreams? One of my dreams was visualizing page after page of text in which I could actually read the words. I wish all my dreams were as obvious in meaning as this one. Is your body trying to tell you something (headaches, stomachaches, tension in the neck, etc.)? Are there song lyrics that just keep popping into your head and you sing them to yourself over and over?

Awareness can lead to life changing insights and can be applicable to all areas on your life: work, personal and professional relationships and overall lifestyle. Awareness can help you identify where you need to make a major decision. It can be a call to action. Quit that job that depresses and stifles you and become self-employed. Go back to school and get the necessary training you need to pursue what you want. End a debilitating or toxic relationship that diminishes you and causes you to experience damaging, negative feelings rather than positive, exhilarating feelings.

Awareness can bring to light the necessity to take the next step, perhaps finding a new relationship or renewing your commitment to an existing relationship. Awareness can make you see the urgency in moving from an environment that doesn't inspire and rejuvenate to one that makes you feel good, that makes you feel grateful, an environment that you look forward to experiencing. Awareness of your core essence can help you understand why you have to change careers. Awareness might allow you to see the joy (and hard work and sacrifice) of having or adopting a child. Awareness can be about personal change and growth. You might discover that you need or desire to become more creative, less judgmental, more loving, less fearful. Awareness is awakening. You begin to pay attention and trust what you are hearing and feeling. All our lives we are taught to conform, we are taught to abandon our intuition, to obey societal imperatives, to allow others to decide what's best for us, to allow others to do our thinking and to make decisions that affect our lives. We are taught to abandon our souls.

Awareness needs to be accorded the highest priority. You need to learn to constantly check in with yourself and make sure you are doing things for the right reasons. Train and discipline yourself to ask those hard, disturbing soul-searching questions:

Is it in my best interest and not a societal imperative in which I feel I must or should?

Is it something you really want to do for yourself? Or are you trying to please your parents or your spouse or to seek some other form of societal approval?

You need to understand why you are doing the things you are doing. These are the types of questions asked by people who have raised their level of awareness:

Why am I practicing the piano two hours

every day? Is it because I am highly competitive and have to be better than everyone else or does playing the piano and improving my skills bring me genuine pleasure?

Is my interest in learning and my "bookworm" type behavior based on natural curiosity or do I have to make high grades (straight A's) to please my parents and to look smart?

Do I enjoy talking to my friends because I love to show how smart I am and really like to put them down by engaging in debates that I know I will win or I am receptive to hear new ideas and different perspectives that I haven't heard or considered?

Did I take that expensive vacation and do all those expensive things to impress my friends and look cosmopolitan or did I really do it for fun and to satiate my curiosity and learn more about my particular areas of interest?

Kathy and I are both history buffs and we recently took a trip to Bismark, North Dakota to visit and see the winter camping site of Lewis and Clark. We had a fabulous time at a very reasonable cost. When we told one of our friends that we went to Bismark. He looked incredulous and remarked "You mean, you went there on purpose?" It was beyond the pale of his imagination that anyone could have a enjoyable vacation in Bismark or any other locale devoid of big time attractions such as theme parks or 5 star restaurants.

Awareness is about living consciously. When you begin living in a state of higher awareness, you begin to question and examine not only the large activities of your life but also the small. Life-long habits that no longer make sense surface in your consciousness. Here is one person's example: all my life I have been putting two packets of sugar into my coffee. I have always opened one, then the other. Today, I found myself placing one packet on top of the other and making one opening operation. Much simpler.

I was preparing to teach a class recently and I inadvertently ripped a page of notes out of a three ring binder. My first instinct was to do what I had always done: search throughout the apartment for a box of those little "paste over the torn hole thingies." I paused and asked myself is there another alternative to searching for a 1/2 hour for something that I might or might not find? Is there another way? I thought why not just put some scotch tape over the hole and re-punch it. That pause and examination of the problem and being open to alternatives is what I call living consciously. Practicing awareness provides you more options and choices. I find it helpful to target areas in my life where I think greater awareness can provide a big payback.

Here are some areas in my life and examples of the benefits that flow from greater awareness:

Awareness of when fear kicks in and creates paralysis or procrastination:

The question I always want answered: Am I not doing something because of some underlying fear or is it that I truly don't want to do it? If I conclude that I really don't want to do something then I need to let go and move on. If I conclude that fear is the culprit that is blocking the road I wish to travel, then I want to do what's necessary to push through the fear and past the blockage. A general guideline for me is whenever I contemplate an action that makes me feel uncomfortable, it's probably something that would be good for me and something I need to do.

Awareness of the patterns that cause friction

between my wife and myself:

Most of time the friction is based on my expectation of what married life should be. Buddha said all suffering is caused by expectations. When I let go of my expectations and focus on the many wonderful benefits (rather than the differences) of being married to Kathy - problem solved and case closed. I need practice in acceptance of perspectives and values that differ from mine. Kathy says that if two of you are exactly alike, one of you isn't necessary. Would you really want to be married to a person exactly like you? It's very painful for me when Kathy (or anybody else) doesn't see things from my perspective. Awareness means seeing things as they really are and this can be painful. As an example, I could characterize my marriage as being a difficult one. However, awareness, though painful, has provided me with the insight that all relationships are hard for me. My wife has hundreds of friends; I can count all my good friends on one hand and have several fingers left over.

Awareness of what risk I am not taking today and why.

Awareness of where assistance and advice is appreciated rather than resented:

I don't want to be like the Boy Scout who helped a little old lady across the street. The only problem was that she didn't want to cross the street.

Awareness about what lessons I can learn from my marriage:

Is Kathy lovable? Immensely so. If I'm having trouble loving Kathy then being loving is something that I really need to work on. Besides bringing immense joy to my life, she also highlights the lessons that I need to work on.

Awareness that I had outgrown the support group that I had attended for 5 years, that it was time to move on:

One of the risks of support groups is the necessity to stay stuck and wounded, the necessity to continually relive your pain and injury to gain sympathy and have a justification for being in the group. What the group often has in common is that they are into talking about recovery rather than going through the hard, sometimes painful, work of actually recovering and growing. It's too easy to "remain in recovery," to remain stuck and never make serious progress in healing. Some never throw away the crutches and learn to walk without support. The risk many support groups run is becoming more of a permanent social club and less of a transitional support group to help you heal and be on your way. The founder of the support group dropped out and I suspect he had reached similar conclusions.

Awareness of how very necessary it is for me to spend 1-2 hours every morning on personal growth and enlightenment. It makes my life works so much better.

Awareness that the class experience is better for both the students and myself when I relate my own personal experiences rather than rely wholly on theory from books. I can teach only what I know and have experienced. The more authentic you are, the better you connect with people.

Awareness about why I was having trouble writing this book: The fear that it wouldn't be acceptable or that I had nothing to say or contribute. This fear of failure was impeding my progress.

Awareness of my self-destructive desire to be myself at all costs (I'm right and the world is wrong syndrome). I am too often unnecessarily controversial and confrontational on insignificant issues that aren't worth the energy of a pitched battle or last stand.

Awareness of my impatience and desire for instant gratification and not being a good sport about doing the work and paying the dues necessary for success, growth and progress.

Once you understand that greater awareness can be learned, you can practice and develop a skill that will really enhance the enjoyment of your life. Here is a suggested list of ways that you can heighten your awareness and practice conscious living:

1) Notice where perfectionism is crippling you. Here is an interesting question to ask yourself: What could you do if you didn't have to do it perfectly? The answer: a great deal more than you are currently doing. Anyone who has ever done any writing knows that you could spend the rest of your life fine tuning your current work in progress. At some point you have to say to yourself, "That's a wrap," let it go and move on. Whenever we look at something in retrospect, we will always have regrets or see ways that it could have been improved. Here is the problem

with perfectionism. We've all heard that the un-examined life is not worth living, but consider too that the unlived life is not worth examining. Perfectionism greatly diminishes the living of life.

2) Notice whether you are living in the past, present or future. The more you can live in the present, the better your life is working. You must have a rigorous relationship with the present moment, because what you put into play today determines how your future will unfold. Ask yourself what do you want your life to look like a year from now and then ask yourself what first step must you take and what new habits must you acquire to head in the proper direction. If you see your-self today as you were in the past, the past is destined to become your future. Don't get dis-couraged because your mind is burdened with regrets about the past or feel guilty about fan-tasies related to the future. We are all afflicted with wandering minds. Nobody can live fully in the present. Even the gurus measure their progress in minutes rather than hours. Julia Ca-maron said, "The quality of life is in proportion, always, to the capacity for delight." The capacity for delight is the gift for paying attention. To pay attention you must be living in the present.

You live in the past when you start too many thoughts with the phrase "if only." What happen yesterday should be as irrelevant to your happi-ness as what happen 10,000 years ago. It's all dead history.

It takes either a certain amount of arrogance or naivete to plan and anticipate the future with any degree of certainty. It's necessary to plan; just don't get upset when life's agenda seems to be different from yours. How do you know you have a future? How do you know that when you leave your house today the wind isn't going to blow a brick off the roof, that hits you in the head? How do you know a meteorite or a dislodged airplane part isn't going to strike you dead? How do you know that a terminal illness isn't going to be detected at your next routine physical examination? You have no ironclad guarantee of a future, much less any certainty as to the details of the future. Life is what happens while you are making other plans. We have all heard the saying "Eat dessert first; life is short." Whenever I hear of someone's life that ends unexpectedly in some bizarre fashion (like being squashed by a piano that fell out of a third story window), I think, "I sure hope he had dessert." The present moment is all that you can count on; make the most of it.

You live in the future, when you start too many thoughts with the phrase "When this ends then everything will be all right." We tend to put off living. "When I lose 20 lbs., then I'll start living." Stephen Leacock said it well:

The child says, "When I am a big boy."
The big boy says, "When I grow up."
The grown up says, "When I get married."
The married say, "When I'm retired."

3) Notice what your first thoughts are when awakening. If they aren't energizing and positive here are some strategies to help you jump-start the day:

a) Take action. Get out of bed and do something; don't lay there and think dark, somber, depressing thoughts. Getting up promptly when I awaken doesn't come easily to me. It's difficult but necessary. (My wife on the other hand leaps out of bed like she has been drinking coffee all night.)

b) Start the day with music or play a tape that inspires or motivates you.

c) Ask yourself a series of questions that force you to see the positive aspects of your life:

   i) What are the good things that I'm looking forward to?

   ii) What am I currently involved in that is exciting?

   iii) What are some possibilities that I might like to explore?

   iv) What are some activities that bring me pleasure?

   v) What am I doing that makes me feel proud?

4) Notice as you prepare for the day, whether you are excited about the day, dread it or is it "just another day." If you seem to be having too many ho-hum, routine, stuck in a rut days, be proactive and try to build something into each day to look forward to:

Having lunch with a friend
Buying or starting a new mystery by your
   favorite author
Window shopping after work for a new
   outfit

Get into the habit of thinking about it before
going to bed and first thing in the morning.
Anticipating pleasure is good for the soul.

5) Notice your thinking: are you a positive thinker
   or a negative thinker? Do you look for the good
   or focus on the problem and whose fault it is? If
   you are a born pessimist, I recommend reading
   *Learned Optimism: How To Change Your Mind &
   Life* by Martin Seligman.

6) Notice what is the most important part of your
   day. Notice what is the most enjoyable part of
   your day. Notice what is the least important part
   of your day. Notice what is the least enjoyable
   part of your day. After you get a handle on
   what's working and what's not working for you,
   you want to search for ways to maximize the
   good and minimize the bad. This exercise made
   me aware that I sometimes, at the end of the day,
   turned on the TV and mindlessly watched whatever was on. This was neither relaxing nor enjoyable; it was merely a bad habit that needed to be
   addressed. I decided to begin videotaping shows
   that would not only be enjoyable to watch but
   could be viewed on my schedule. Another perk
   to watching videotapes is that you can fast forward through the commercials.

7) Notice what it is you willingly set aside every-

thing else to do. I discovered that I really enjoy being with my wife and was comfortable following her agenda. She gets to pick the restaurants we eat in, the movies we view and the vacations we take. This isn't a sacrifice. We have similar interests and I just enjoy hanging out with her.

8) Notice whether money is a problem or a joy for you. Do you have a healthy relationship with money? Is it to be spent or to be hoarded? Are you in debt? Are your credit cards maxed out? I think one of the fundamental secrets to money management and eliminating financial stress and worry is simply to live within your means.

9) Notice the kinds of people you spend time with. Do you feel more alive around them or do you feel bored or drained? If you want to be creative, hang around creative people. If you want to be happy, hang around happy people. If you want to be productive, hang around productive people. Don't expect support from people who are stuck in toxic, dysfunctional behavior that they know and are comfortable with. Any recovering alcoholic will tell you that he can't expect his friends from the local pub to celebrate and support his sobriety. How can they, when they are in a state of denial about their own drinking.

10) Notice the types of people you are attracted to and for what reasons.

11) Notice who and when you are trying to impress.

12) Notice your surroundings. Do they support you? Your surroundings can make you feel

inspired and creative or depressed and lethargic. We experience places almost the way we do people. Some places we love at first sight and other places make us uncomfortable.

13) Notice how you feel when someone asks you what type of work you do? Are proud, shamed or indifferent?

14) Notice whether spirituality is important to you. How much time do you give it during the day? Is the concept of a higher power meaningful to you? Do you put more energy into trusting or doubting and worrying? My take on spirituality is that I'm part of something much bigger than my own needs and this bigness has to be honored even though not fully understood.

15) Notice how your body feels. Are you tense and worn out or are you energetic?

16) Notice the times and conditions when your energy is at a peak level. I'm a morning person and that is when my energy is consistently high. I schedule my creative efforts to coincide with peak energy levels and do the rote things (pay bills, return phone calls, run errands, etc.) in the afternoon.

17) Notice moments when you feel fully alive. I feel alive when I'm taking a risk and stepping out of my comfort zone. I feel alive when I'm being creative and in touch with my potential and the possibilities of life. I feel alive when I'm living in the present and paying attention. (Someone once said that God is in the details.) When I'm taking

my early morning walk during the summer and have a heightened sense of awareness, I observe more. I will frequently notice a new wild flower or birds I haven't seen before.

18) Notice which activities move you to give nothing less than your best.

19) Notice where your passion lies. What creates real enthusiasm for you?

20) Notice what you appreciate, what makes you happy, what fills you with delight (however small), what makes you feel energized and optimistic, what action and experiences make you feel as if you count in your own eyes. Special moments that I really treasure are those where I feel I have really connected with someone. I am always looking for ways to make this happen. I have discovered that, though it sometimes makes me feel uncomfortable because intimacy isn't my strong suit, being authentic, doing small loving, real acts and being willing to go first (acknowledging the other person, smiling, beginning the conversation) break down barriers and allow intimacy to occur. It also makes it much easier to connect with people when I view strangers as friends I haven't yet made.

21) Notice who you put first. Notice who you put last.

22) Notice what you pay attention to.

23) Notice when you give your power away. Is it with encounters with the opposite sex? Do

controlling people intimidate you?

24) Notice what makes you feel loved? Notice what makes your partner feel loved?

25) Notice what you do that makes you feel nurtured. How many ways do you have to nurture yourself?

One problem many of us face is that we have a limited repertoire of healthy ways to celebrate life's little victories. We have been conditioned to equate overeating and overdrinking with celebration. Some of the institutionalized ways corporate America rewards employees and some of the other celebratory practices in the workplace really need to be examined. Is the annual Christmas party really that much fun and do you really enjoy participating in those monthly pot luck lunches where everyone brings something and it's practically impossible to eat sensibly? We get a promotion or increase in salary or complete a major project and feel like we have the world by the tail. We feel good and understandably want to celebrate. Is your first instinct to have a night on the town, go party and get drunk or celebrate by dining out and wind up overeating and overspending?

You want to develop awareness about the experiences that you really enjoy and have them mentally on call so that when celebration is appropriate you have a list of choices that really work for you. I will share a couple of examples. I consider a hot shower in the middle of the day an excellent way to take a well-deserved break. When I complete a task, I will reward myself by browsing in a bookstore and possibly buying a book. If I have had a very productive day and have accomplished my goals, a little nap isn't out of the question. These are small rewards for small victories, but I find them healthier and much more nurturing than restless snacking or going out for a candy bar in the middle of the afternoon.

26) Notice when you are being real and when you are being phony and posturing. You aren't real when you present a false image to others and never let the real you shine through. Like one-dimensional characters, phonies play-act through life instead of really living it. When you don't allow the real self to shine through, you use an enormous amount of energy maintaining that facade. You pay a big price for not being real, especially if you are never real. It's OK to show genuine like (or disappointment) in your daily interactions with other people. I spend a lot of time in our local Barnes & Noble. I really enjoy the experience and like the people that work there. I'm not shy or reserved about my enjoyment and it's a day brightener for all. The real you is much more attractive than the phony you. The real you is very lovable and very powerful.

27) Notice when you overeat. If I buy a bag of potato chips, I will eat the entire bag in one sitting. There are some foods that I am powerless around and I acknowledge that and I just don't bring them in the house. I also know that once something is on my plate it's history. I have to be selective about which restaurants I frequent. There is an excellent steak house nearby that serves gargantuan portions. Whenever I used to

eat there, I always felt like I violated one of Miss Piggy's rules on dining. Miss Piggy says never eat more than you can lift. This awareness gives me control over my eating and allows me to eat sensibly without having to fight daily, losing battles with temptation.

28) Notice whether your clothes make you feel self-conscious or allow you to be comfortable with yourself.

I practically live in tennis shoes and discovered that when they got beyond the point of being presentable, I would try to hide my feet. I was unknowingly self-conscious about this part of my appearance. Any apparel that attacks your self-esteem needs to be tossed.

29) Notice when you feel anxious or stressed out. Pay attention to what you do during the stressful times in your day. Do you head for the refrigerator, even though you are not hungry? Do you pick up the phone and call your boyfriend/husband to see if he really loves you? Do you obsess about the company you would start if you had the resources, or the book you would write if you had the time, or the traveling you would do if you had the money? Notice any distraction that takes you away from the action or result you desire. Notice when your thoughts wander. Notice what was happening just before they strayed. Often our thoughts wander when we are faced with an emotion we're trying to avoid. Be aware of your thoughts as they hunt for somewhere to focus rather than on the task at hand.

30) Notice what your body language says. Words are only about 8% of communication. The rate of speech, tonal inflection, facial gestures and body language are the true communicators. When I teach the *Dare To Date* class, I always say: ***If you don't look approachable you won't be approached.*** Even though you may want a relationship, if your body language says STAY THE HELL AWAY FROM ME, you aren't going to have much success. My wife had unknowingly perfected negative body language that contributed to a total lack of success in dating. The pattern didn't change until she was in her forties. Here are some specific ways to develop positive body language that can help develop relationships:

Practice smiling.

Practice having warm and positive thoughts about the opposite sex. If you either fear or hate the opposite sex, you body language will betray you.

Practice being gracious and charming. Next time you go to a social function pretend to be the host rather than the guest.

You may desire companionship and warmth, but if your unconscious intentions and behavior is to keep people at a distance, the experiences of separation and pain will surface again and again until you come to understand that you are the culprit.

31) Notice when your significant other irritates you.

Are there patterns of actions or events that frequently lead to conflict?

Are you each comfortable with the other's driving? Kathy and I used to both terrify each other (for different reasons) when driving in the mountains. I had to learn to respect Kathy's fear and drive more cautiously. Kathy had to understand that driving too slowly would cause other drivers to take chances and pass on curves.

32) Notice when you rain on your own parade. Are you the type that looks a gift horse in the mouth? You want to practice enjoying, rather than questioning in a negative manner.

33) Notice how bountiful life is. If this isn't apparent to you, read about life under Stalin in the 1930's or the concentration camp experiences of the holocaust survivors or listen to stories of the depression from your parents or grandparents. Rent and view Schindler's List.

34) Notice how much freedom you experience in life.

Freedom of movement
Freedom from religious persecution
Freedom from arbitrary imprisonment
Freedom of thought and expression
Freedom to be the best you can be

35) Notice if you notice.

Fear

**Life shrinks or expands in
proportion to one's courage.**

Anais Nin

We all need to ask ourselves whether we want to live in
the direction of our fears or in the direction of our dreams.

When I'm not making progress in the direction that I
think I want to go, I ask myself, is it because I really don't
wish to travel the path in question or is it that I'm blocked
and paralyzed by some fear? If fear gets the nod, then I select
and practice a fear reducing technique that allows me to
move forward. Whenever you are feeling stuck, procrastinat-
ing or wallowing in indecision you are probably being held
hostage by fear.

The kind of fear I'm referring to isn't fear brought
about by danger or life threatening situations. I'm talking
about the fears that keep us from taking sensible risks, from
pursuing our goals and dreams, from getting what we want
out of life. Fears that don't allow us to just plain be happy.

Fear can permeate every nook and cranny of our existence. I have learned through teaching the *Dare To Date*
course that the biggest obstacle and hurdle to dating is the
fear of rejection. This is the fear that prevents people from

initiating social contact, making small talk, asking for a first date or even sending the signals that its OK for the other person to ask for a date.

By re-educating the mind, you can learn to accept fear as simply a fact of life rather than as a barrier to success. The difference between those who get on with their lives and those that remain stuck is their understanding and attitude towards fear. People who are growing and realizing their potential have learned how to coexist with their fear. They do not allow fear to dominate their lives and create crippling paralysis. Madam Curie said, "Nothing in life is to be feared. It is only to be understood." Franklin D. Roosevelt said, "We have nothing to fear, but fear itself." Learning how to co-exist with your fear allows you to take action. Whenever you take action, the fear diminishes. When fear begins to diminish, you will see the world as a less threatening and more joyful place. Unmanaged and misunderstood fears keep us on the sidelines of life rather than allowing us to go in there, mix it up and participate fully. Fear can diminish your life in so many ways:

> Fear keeps you from asserting yourself and naming your desires. It persuades you to set easier goals and gives you permission to do less than you are capable. Fear convinces you to settle for less instead of going for more.

> Fear reduces creativity, preventing you from acting on or even considering all the options and choices available to you in life.

> Fear of failing causes indecisiveness and confusion that prevents you from taking reasonable and necessary risks which are needed to grow and enjoy life.

Fear of appearing vulnerable keeps you from asking for help or benefiting from support and helping hands offered by others.

Fear is the ultimate God we appease by developing dysfunctional habits that keep us from having to confront the new and to seriously consider the possibility of real change. Fear triggers all the defense systems that you have carefully nurtured and built up over the years.

Fear keeps you on a path, filled with deep dissatisfying ruts, that forces you to go in a joyless direction.

Fear makes us quitters and doesn't allow us to give life our best shot.

Fear makes you give up just one step short of your goal, instead of going that final mile or climbing that last hill.

Our fears know no boundaries. We fear the inevitable: aging, children leaving home (some might consider this a blessing rather than a fear), illness, accidents, loss and dying. Woody Allen says he doesn't fear death; he just doesn't want to be there when it happens. We fear the possibilities of catastrophes: nuclear wars, rape, floods and fire. We fear being decisive and taking action: going back school, changing careers, retiring, making new friends, relocating, divorcing or ending a relationship. We fear things that attack our ego: rejection, failure, disapproval, loss of image or looking foolish. Fear of failure is the single greatest obstacle to success. It prevents you from taking that first step that places you in uncharted territory, that slippery feeling turf that's outside your comfort zone. It is fear that cripples us and doesn't allow us to fulfill our potential.

A book could be written listing the millions of things that create and trigger fear. The insight that you need to grasp is that the myriad fears that our minds can conjure up all have a common denominator. All fears can be reduced to one simple premise: you feel that you can't handle the outcome of a particular experience or situation.You feel overwhelmed and fear that you can't handle whatever life is presenting you. The truth is that you can and you do. Excessive fear means that you are not trusting your coping abilities and aren't feeling very good about yourself.

We always underestimate our coping abilities. Ask yourself three questions. Have you ever had a relationship problem? Have you ever had a financial problem? Finally, have you ever had a health problem? We have all had these problems. A large percentage of us have been divorced; many of us have lost jobs for a variety of reasons and we have all been to the doctor. We have all encountered various problems in life and yet somehow we survive. None of them are show stoppers; the sun always comes up the next day. The experiences might not have been pleasant, but you survived.

When we are in the midst of a crises or unpleasant situation, our perceptions are warped and we fail to trust our coping skills. When you discover that you really can handle anything that comes your way, when you come to accept that you can handle all the curve balls that life throws you, what then do you have to fear? NOTHING.

I once had an overwhelming fear of public speaking and finally developed the courage to do something about it. I joined Toastmasters. Toastmasters provides a nurturing and supportive environment for those who know this fear and want to push beyond it.

The first speech given is called the "Ice Breaker"; you talk for 5 minutes about yourself. How bad can that be?

After all, it's the one subject you should be a leading expert on. But fear is irrational and you are still nervous when you get up to give that first talk. I have a habit of writing everything on yellow legal size pads of paper and leave half-used yellow legal pads strewn all over the place. When I approached the podium to give my first speech in front my toastmaster friends, I glanced at my notes and the first couple of lines read "two boxes of spaghetti, loaf of French bread and one jar of pasta sauce." I had picked up the wrong legal pad and had my grocery-shopping list instead of the notes for my talk. Panic set in; I prayed for a trap door in the floor to open up and swallow me whole. That didn't happen. I gave the speech and guess what - the world didn't end!

Fear makes us consider worst case scenarios and exaggerate what is going to happen if things don't go as planned. Life never proceeds as planned. The secret is not to let that reality prevent you from living life. You really can handle the outcome or consequences of any action. There is no greater thrill or feeling of exhilaration than to meet a fear head on, do battle and defeat something that's been limiting and crippling you all your life. One of the sentiments frequently echoed at Toastmasters by members who have found the courage to stand up and give that first speech is "why did I wait so long to do this?" Once you do what you fear, the fear is reduced and no longer has that paralyzing control over you.

A salesman (we will call him Mike) dreaded company meetings where he might be called on by the president to say a few words in front of the sales force about what was happening in his sales territory. He would begin to become depressed, frightened and scared months before the annual year-end meeting of the sales force. His first talk at Toastmasters was life transforming. It gave him an immeasurable amount of self-confidence and joy. He went on to participate in regional contests and did very well. I know the feeling.

We pay a tremendous price, if we allow ourselves to be defined and limited by our fears. Susan Jeffers in her wonderful book *Feel The Fear And Do It Anyway* lists 5 very profound insights about fear. I carry this list in my wallet and refer to it whenever I sense that fear is blocking my path.

1. THE FEAR WILL NEVER GO AWAY AS LONG AS YOU CONTINUE TO GROW

Whenever you step outside your comfort zone, fear will be your companion. The good news is that every time you step outside your comfort zone, your comfort zone expands.

The flip side of this insight is that if you are never experiencing any fear, you are never stepping outside of your comfort zone. You are stuck big time!

Somebody once asked me, "Why do you want to go around feeling scared all the time?" You don't. But what's the alternative? If you aren't willing to risk the discomfort of stepping outside your comfort zone, you will remain in a perpetual life-long state of being stuck. You will suffer chronic dissatisfaction that can lead to mild or low-grade depression. You will always view the world in dreary black and white, rather than in living color. You will never allow yourself to consider exciting possibilities in a meaningful and real way. You will never experience the exhilaration of conquering a fear.

When surveys are conducted to identify what are the most common fears, public speaking ranks right up there near the top. Barbara Sher (author of *Wishcraft*) makes this point in her seminars by saying she is going to ask someone in the audience to come up and give a 7 minute talk on their views on personal growth. Everybody that has a fear of public speaking turns ashen white. You don't understand the crippling power of fear until it's actually confronted.

2. THE ONLY WAY TO GET RID OF THE FEAR OF

DOING SOMETHING IS TO GO OUT AND DO IT

If I were to recommend 5 books on public speaking and you bought all 5 books, underlined all the meaningful passages and took copious notes, you would still have a fear of public speaking. You can't read yourself through fear; you can't think yourself through fear; you can't "seminar" your way through fear. The only way to get beyond the fear is to do what you are afraid of. We all want the fear to go away first and then we will do it. This is "cart before the horse" thinking. You must take action before the fear goes away.

3. THE ONLY WAY TO FEEL BETTER ABOUT YOURSELF IS TO GO OUT AND DO IT.

I am not saying that you will be clinically depressed for the rest of your life, if you aren't willing to face your fears and deal with them effectively. What I am saying is that you will be confined to a life of mediocrity. You will always live in this middle gray zone where life isn't really too bad, it just isn't that great. It guarantees a ho-hum existence. You will never feel that excitement of achieving your potential. George Bernard Shaw puts it this way, "Far better is it to dare to do great things, to win glorious triumphs even though checkered by failure, rather than join the ranks of those poor miserable souls who neither suffer much nor enjoy much, for they live in gray dim twilight that neither knows victory nor defeat."

4. NOT ONLY AM I GOING TO EXPERIENCE FEAR WHENEVER I'M ON UNFAMILIAR GROUND, BUT SO IS EVERYONE ELSE

Fear can be a very shaming emotion. Friends will say to us "That shouldn't scare you" or "Don't be such an old fraidy cat" or you will say to yourself "I shouldn't be afraid of that." Shame is a crippling emotion. It's the belief that you are defective. When you understand that fear is a universal emotion and comes with the territory of being alive, you no longer need to feel defective or inadequate. It just means that you need to develop the skill to identify and manage your fears effectively. People who get on with their lives have better strategies for managing and co-existing with their fears.

Fear cripples and this is why you need a sense of urgency about understanding your fears and learning how deal with them effectively.

5. PUSHING THROUGH FEAR IS LESS FRIGHTEN-ING THAN LIVING WITH THE UNDERLYING FEAR THAT COMES FROM A FEELING OF HELPLESSNESS.

Conquering fear allows you to approach life with confidence.

Let's review some ways and techniques to help you reduce and push through your fears:

Understand and apply the power of accountability. We often have good intentions, but we aren't very good at holding ourselves accountable. The failure to keep New Year's resolutions highlights the difficulties with self-accountability. We come up with all kinds of silly and convoluted reasons why we didn't do what we intended or promised ourselves that we would do. If this rings true with you, consider turning the reins of accountability over to someone else. If you have a trusted friend, you would say to that friend, "Nancy, by Friday, I plan to do X, Y and Z." On Friday, Nancy would ask you whether you did those things. Nancy would hold you accountable. This process of letting someone else hold you accountable feels psychologically binding and there is a greater probability that you would will do what needs to be done. Savvy "self helpers" often form accountability groups that meet regularly. Everyone tells what specific actions they plan to take. At the next meeting, each person reports their progress for the past period and their plans for the next period. You discover it is easier to do the planned tasks rather than trying to convince the group that your flimsy, transparent excuses are valid. It's a very powerful process.

Another possibility is to make a written contract with yourself saying what you plan to do by a specific date. Sign and date the contract. This will be more of a real commitment and feel more binding.

The size and complexity of a large task can be overwhelming and intimidating. Whatever is undefined is not understood and the lack of understanding is what creates the fear. The secret is to break a large, scary and undefined project into smaller, well-defined, manageable parts. Sydney Harris author of *Winners & Losers* said "A winner takes a big problem and separates it into smaller parts so that it can be more easily manipulated; a loser takes a lot of little problems and rolls them together until they are unsolvable." If one of these smaller parts still scares you, break that component into smaller parts until all the parts are small enough that you feel comfortable. Then do the first task.

The action of starting will make you feel good and give you the confidence to do the next step. Confidence doesn't mean the total elimination of fear. Confidence allows you to manage and control your fear. Action makes us focus on the task at hand rather than worry about all the things that can go wrong in the future. If you do nothing, you become preoccupied with your negative thoughts. Don't worry about starting slowly; just start. Begin with baby steps when learning a new skill. It's OK to be a beginner. Trust the process. Proceed at your own pace, the more you do, the more your confidence will develop and the faster your progress will be. You will take larger more confident steps as you progress towards your desired goal. After you have done several steps, you will feel the momentum grow, your confidence will increase; you are on a roll.

I am an advocate of using personal ads for meeting people. I met my wife through the personals. Writing a personal ad, calling up strangers and going out on first date generates all kinds of fears (What if the guy is a serial killer? Will I be rejected? Am I attractive enough? Do I have anything interesting to say? etc.). One of the exercises students do in my *Dare To Date* class is to write a personal ad. You should hear the groans. Not only do they have to write it, they have to read it aloud and get feedback from myself and class members. The experience is always positive. The initial action of taking that first step creates confidence and excitement. Class members feel good and are pleasantly surprised by how supportive the class is and how well received their ad is. Many of the students, sometimes the next day, submit the ad. Having people respond to your ad, having people express interest and wanting to meet you is good for the soul and great for your self-esteem. It generates the courage and confidence needed to pick up that phone, call a stranger and meet for a cup of coffee.

Every step taken creates confidence and lessens the fear.

When I was moving into Kathy's condo, she wanted me to paint all the rooms. I had all kinds of great reasons and exquisite rationalizations why the apartment didn't need painting. (I like an apartment that looks lived in and peeling paint certainly gives that impression; we might be moving in 5-10 years, can't we hang on for just another decade; if I paint the place, we are going to have to endure that smell of fresh paint; who knows, future studies may show that paint smells might cause weight on the hips!) I pulled out all stops. A defense lawyer would have been proud of my tortured reasoning and closing arguments.

The real issue was that I was scared that I would make a mess of the project and get paint all over the place. I belong to a Saturday morning support group and had enough awareness to understand that at the root of my procrastination and delaying tactics was my fear of being incompetent and making a big ole mess. I suspect that I also thought that this wouldn't be the coolest thing to do to impress my new love. I presented the problem to the group and asked for some help and guidance. They asked some very deep questions and said some very profound things. Someone asked if I had bought the paint and a paintbrush. "Uh, No," but that was something I sure could do. I brought the paint and the brush and eagerly awaited Saturday for some more guidance. "What's next?" I wanted to know. Well, the next step, some one said, was to take the paint lid off the can, dip the brush into the paint and make a mark on the wall. I can do that, I thought. "What's the next step?" I asked. Well, dip the brush into the paint again and make a second mark.

Being a college grad, I was beginning to sense a pattern; they were onto something that just might work. It was really as simple as that. The fear vanished when I took action and started. I needed no further help after starting the project.

Be your own shrink. "Nobody knows the trouble I've seen" as one song puts it; nobody knows your life history and your issues better than you do. A counselor is really just a catalyst. You have to do all the heavy lifting. You have to take the ultimate responsibility for your life and happiness if any real progress is to be made.

Asking yourself probing, soul-searching questions can help you gain awareness about a fear and understand what needs to be done. Remember that good questions always lead to more good questions and the by-product of a good question is good information. Asking the right questions is cheaper than psychotherapy and it's so much more convenient (no traveling across town, no making appointments and waiting in the outer office with all the other "disturbed" people). Here are some questions you might want to ask yourself:

What is my fear about?

What am I afraid of?

What is the worst possible outcome?
If my fear is on the surface, what lies underneath?

Is the fear truly about the present experience or does it gain power by evoking some related past experience?

How is my fear protecting me and do I still need that protection?

How could I be made to feel safer, while moving beyond my fear?

What can I do to get out of my fear and into my creativity (i.e. problem solving mode)?

If someone else were telling me about this fear, what advice would I give him or her? This is a very powerful question. We often know what we need to do, but lack the courage to take that first step.

There is an effective fear reducing strategy called anchoring to a previous positive experience. Unfortunately we obsess on the experiences that re-enforce our fearful thinking. We are conditioned to think in negative and limiting ways. Our disempowering thoughts (thoughts that aren't good for us) create an emotional climate that is ideal for fears to grow, fester and become unmanageable and crippling. Make a conscious effort to connect with and relive relevant, previous positive experiences. Our past victories and successes can be used to create confidence.

When I first began to teach and do public speaking, it was a terrifying experience for me. The predominant thought would be "Just who the hell do you think you are? Who told you that you had anything new or worthwhile to say?" To counterbalance those thoughts, I would consciously think positive thoughts and mentally relive prior positive experiences related to public speaking. I would think about the Toastmaster speech contests that I had won and all the wonderful, positive feedback I had received from members in my Toastmasters Club. I would get in touch and refocus on why I was teaching. It's my belief that nothing is more fulfilling and worthwhile than service and I know that my life works better when I'm a loving person and share what I have learned.

This strategy of anchoring to a positive emotional state can be applied to any area of your life. In my class, *How To Leave The Job You Hate And Find The Life You Love*, I encounter many people who are stuck and remain in jobs that create dissatisfaction and chronic frustration rather than joy and optimism. I remind these people that their mind is being controlled and dominated by their negative thinking and they need to get in touch with their positive experiences related to their work.

I ask them to review their work history and consider the following: someone thought enough of their abilities to hire them rather than others who applied for the same job. If they received pay raises and promotions, they must have some skills and competencies that are in demand. If they received "thanks" and other votes of approval from superiors, people they worked with and customers who were appreciative of good service, they must be capable of doing a good job. Getting in touch with positive experiences will increase your confidence and prod you into the necessary action for change: updating your resume or making that appointment for a job interview. The anchoring to positive experiences technique allows us to see the possibilities that aren't apparent when you are totally absorbed by negative thinking and fear. Fear distorts reality.

Thinking Big

**There are two ways you can die.
You can stop breathing
or you can stop dreaming.**

Rocco Casciato

It's unhealthy not to have dreams and aspirations. The bigger the dreams, the more alive and excited you are. Dreams are good for us. Dreams tell us who we could and would be, it we have the courage to listen and pursue our desires. It's a good mental health practice. There is a high correlation between the lack of dreams and depression. We stay stuck when we don't dream big enough. We don't allow ourselves to see all the wondrous possibilities that life has to offer.

Thinking big can help put new projects into a less overwhelming perspective. As a beginning writer, I allowed myself to have the goal of writing a book a year for the next 10 years. This made the current book writing project less scary, more manageable and reframes the present endeavor as merely a stepping stone to greater things.

A book that I really find stimulating is *The Wish List* by Barbara Ann Kipfer. It lists approximately 6,000 wishes, fantasies, hopes and dreams. I periodically go through it and check the entries that intrigue and excite me and ask myself "why not?" and "if not now, when?" It's an excellent source of inspiration. I often add checked entries to my own "things that I want to do" list.

In career counseling sessions, clients' self-imposed limitations surface all the time. We have difficulty facing and confronting our own potential. Dreams force us to consider abandoning the comfortable ruts that we have settled in as we travel through life. We need to understand and acknowledge how hard change is. Staying stuck is a learned defense mechanism. Change (new thoughts, new action, new behavior) is uncomfortable, especially in the early stages. If it were fun, change would be easy instead of a struggle, and everyone would be doing it. Most people shy away from change unless it's forced on them by circumstance. It's a small percentage of people that truly examine their lives and decide to undertake action that will lead to significant change. The vast majority of people let inertia rule. They follow the path of least resistance.

The avoidance of change, on a short-term basis, makes sense. Why change? Why do this sometimes painful soul searching and take action that makes you feel uncomfortable? But on a longer-term basis, staying stuck creates a feeling of staleness, a feeling that your life really isn't working and something is lacking. Once you gain awareness about this and understand the dynamics of change. You learn to take action and make decisions that may generate initial discomfort, but in the long term allows you to grow and have a better life.

I encounter many competent, highly skilled and talented people who are being paid far less than what their talents are worth on the open market. When confronted with this reality, they defensively say "But that's what I'm worth" or "That's what I'm currently being paid" or "I've never made more than this amount." They refuse to recognize their potential, because to contemplate their potential requires unsettling thoughts, unfamiliar behavior and new patterns that cause discomfort. If I encounter this roadblock with a client, I always say, "Humor me, lets pretend you are worth a lot more than you are currently making. What would your resume look like and what would you do differently?" These types of questions force us to think, to view ourselves differently and to consider our potential in a real way. This awareness can lead to newfound confidence that allows one to pursue higher paying and higher quality jobs. It usually results in the procurement of a position in which the pay is more in alignment with the individual's our true worth. As Les Brown says, "Shoot for the moon. Even if you miss, you land in the stars." We are highly programmable creatures. If you believe you are only worth a certain amount, you are right; it's a self-fulfilling prophecy. On the other hand, if you really believe that you are worth substantially more, you are also correct.

Be aware of self-imposed limitations and ceilings that inhibit your growth and career advancement. When I decided to adhere to the philosophy of doing what I love and trusting that the money would follow, I honestly could not initially see how I could make more than a meager income. I set very low financial goals for myself. I discovered that when I reached a goal, I plateaued at my self-imposed financial ceiling and remained stuck there. I decided to think big and increase my financial goals by a factor of 10. What I discovered was that I again encountered the same problem. I reached my goal and plateaued. In order to continue growing, you have to continually raise the bar and set higher goals.

It's important that your goals are consistent with your values and definition of integrity or your success will deplete rather than fulfill you. I'm not willing to abandon the path that provides passion and creativity to make an excessive amount of money. Greed (pursuing what you really don't need) creates rather than solves problems.

Vagueness And Generalities: Enemies Of Personal Growth

He who wants to do everything will never do anything.

Andre Maurois

Dreams are necessary to sustain us and allow us to see what is possible. Dreams create feelings of exhilaration. But are dreams enough? Dreams without progress create frustration, anxiety and resentment. It's no good to see the good life without being able to participate.

To make real progress towards any goal in life you have to deal with specifics. You have to have specific goals and take specific action within a specific time frame. If not, you have chosen to disregard the power of focus. If you dream of being rich without any clarity or precision, you will probably just fantasize about wealth all your life without any palpable progress. Having a specific goal in mind (e.g., save $1,000 by the end of the year), dramatically increases the probability of success. If you are living your life without specific goals, you have made a commitment to aimless floundering rather than the pursuit of excellence and achievement. It's important to write down your specific goals. It helps you clarify what you want and it's harder to ignore written goals. Mental goals just don't feel as psychologically binding; we are more serious about written goals. In the early fifties, a study was undertaken at a prestigious university to evaluate the success of a specific graduating class. Twenty years later in follow up interviews, it was discovered that the 3% with written goals had amassed greater financial wealth that the other 97%.

Why are written goals so effective? All of our personal history and living experiences exist in our memory. We only have access to a very small percentage of that knowledge or "knowing" in the waking conscious state. Methods exist (hypnosis, dreams, etc.) that help us delve deeply into the subconscious or unconscious realms and retrieve experiences. Specificity provides the focus and precision that allows us access to more knowledge and relevant past life experience. It allows the subconscious to marshal seldom used resources (forgotten memories and experiences) to assist you. Just remember you are smarter than you think. It's learning to define what we want in concrete, specific terms that allows us to access that "hidden" knowledge.

The clarity and precision provided by specific and targeted thinking is also beneficial in monitoring and evaluating progress. I constantly examine my life searching for adjustments or fine tuning that can help me enjoy my life more fully and align my daily living strategies with my dreams and goals. I want to stay on track and not waste time and energy.

I have a criterion for successful living and employ a feedback mechanism to evaluate how my life is working. I use two perspectives to view and manage my life. The overall general evaluation is done at a macro level. The specifics are managed at a micro level.

At the macro level, I have 4 indicators that signal to me how my life it working. They are like the red light in your car that begins to blink indicating that you are low on oil and need to take immediate action. When one of these 4 indicators begins to blink, I feel a sense of urgency that compels me to pay attention, get in touch with my feelings and gain awareness about what is going on:

SERENITY OR ANXIETY INDICATOR: Whenever my serenity is diminished, I want to understand why I'm allowing it to slip away. I don't mean temporary disappointment or momentary fleeting feelings of anger, fear, etc. If I'm out of kilter for more than couple of hours, I want to know what's causing my prolonged anxiety and take steps to remedy it.

LIFESTYLE INDICATOR: I lead a fairly health life combining moderate exercise with sensible eating habits. If I catch myself getting a candy bar out of a vending machine at 3:00 in the afternoon, I know (red light flashing) that there is some stress or worry that I'm not handling properly.

ENTHUSIASM OR DEPRESSION INDICATION: Kathy and I are always saying, "life is good". When you believe that life is indeed good, you can take on the day with enthusiasm. If I am not emotionally up and going through the day with enthusiasm, I have the awareness to recognize this and I'll take immediate action to alter my emotional state. Temporary low moods are normal and are experienced by all. I'm talking about prolonged feeling of the blahs or mild depression. I know nothing good ever comes of depression.

CREATIVITY INDICATOR: We are all highly creative. When answers to life's problems are not forthcoming or alternatives never enter my mind and I'm feeling stuck; I know there is something blocking my creativity. I will do exercises to stimulate my mind and get the creative juices flowing. Creativity is to some degree a learned skill and can be jump started and sustained.

I have learned (the hard way) the value of quickly identifying when non-productive and energy-draining mental states occur. Developing awareness of these emotional states allows me the option of responding quickly and choosing strategies to change how I feel. For many, being stressed out, worried, giving away their serenity or not using their creativity skill to problem solve has become a depressing, expected way of life. These people do not routinely check in on how they are feeling and have no criteria as to whether they are experiencing life the way they wish to.

At the micro level, I try to manage all aspects of my life with a specific criterion that tells me whether that particular component is working satisfactorily. I have listed some areas of my life and the criteria that I used to judge how well they are working:

RELATIONSHIP WITH MY WIFE: Out of sight, out of mind (except for thoughts of love). When I'm with my wife, I want to thoroughly enjoy her company. When I am teaching or socializing with my friends, I want to be fully present. If thoughts of an earlier argument (lets call that a spirited debate) I had with my wife begins to seep into my consciousness, I feel that our relationship isn't working optimally. The problem needs to be resolved quickly. I don't want to carry around lingering resentments in a passive aggressive way.

RELATIONSHIP WITH MY CHIL-DREN: This is effective but not a fun one to think about. I ask myself how would I feel if something happened to one of my kids. Obviously I would feel a lot of pain and grief because I love my kids. If I also had feelings of guilt when I asked this question, this tells me that there is some unfinished business. There is something I could be doing and I'm not doing it. It might just be that I'm taking them for granted and I need to call them on the phone and tell them how much I love them. This is a wonderful criterion to use because it allows a second chance and affords me the opportunity act while there is time. If I feel no guilt when asking this question, then I'm satisfied with my role in the relationship.

VOCATION/JOB: This is an easy one. I can't wait for every day to start. My philosophy is do what you love and the money will follow. When my passion for an activity wanes and it becomes drudgery, I honor my existing commitments and phase that activity out of my life and pursue my current interests and passions.

LIFESTYLE: Is it reasonably healthy and also enjoyable? I try to build types of exercise into my life that I truly enjoy. Walking always brings my enjoyment. Running or using a treadmill doesn't work for me. I have always wondered about the priorities of people who exercise on a treadmill and then drive two blocks to the corner grocery store to pick up a quart of milk. I eat healthy and maintain a low-fat diet most of the time. This is easy when dining at home or having a quick lunch at Subway. When special occasions arise or I'm dining out with my wife at a nice restaurant, the healthy eating has to be balanced with enjoyment and that might include a calorie-laden dessert. It's all about balance and finding a lifestyle in which feelings of deprivation are kept to a minimum. If I always ate healthy and never allowed for celebration, I would feel like a martyr rather than a person who is enjoying life. Martyrdom has never worked for me; striving for balance between enjoyment and health is for me the key to long term success.

FRIENDS: People are either nutritious and good for you or toxic and bad for you. You can tell by how people make you feel. There are people that make you feel good, support you and bring out the best in you. These are the people you want to associate with. If someone's presence always triggers some negative emotion (fear, worry, anger, insecurity, hopelessness, frustration, etc.) that's a toxic person for you. I make it a rule to seek out nutritional people and avoid toxic people. Ask yourself some specific questions to determine whether it is in your best interest to either begin or continue the relationship:

Does this person energize you?
Does this person make you laugh?
Does this person motivate and inspire you?
Is this person a good listener?
Does this person allow you to be yourself?

One of my wife's friends (Barbara Winter, author of *How To Make A Living Without A Job)* had an interesting comment on friendships. Do you spend a significant amount of time with someone for whom you would not think of buying a $5.00 gift? You want to learn to fly with the eagles rather than scratch in the dirt with the turkeys.

READING: Is it fulfilling and rewarding or are you just killing time? I used to read two newspapers in the morning, read Time and Newsweek and listen to McNeil Lehrer (an hour-long news show) Monday through Friday. I realized most of this was done by habit rather than for enjoyment. I was getting the same news 5 times and 90% of what was being reported was negative and didn't contribute to my life in a positive way. I awoke and realized my time could be put to a more joyful use.

I love to read and I knew that breaking the habit of reading stories with negative content would not be easy. Abruptly stopping a bad habit creates a void that increases the possibility of a relapse. It's a much more effective and easier strategy to replace a bad habit with a good habit.

I now limit myself to reading the sports section in one paper in the morning. I no longer read Time or Newsweek and I watch McNeil selectively. To fill the vacuum created by this reduced reading, I asked my wife, who is a librarian and knows my reading tastes, to help me out and to make sure that I always have a pile of good books next to my reading chair. In the morning you will now find me engrossed in a good book rather than mindlessly and routinely reading the newspaper. If you enjoy reading, a good practice is to immediately start another book after finishing a good read. This habit will assure that you will always be in the middle of a good book; one of life's greatest pleasures for a reader. I also carry a good book with me and read whenever unexpected delays create down time. I don't have to read a two-year-old Reader's Digest with the cover torn off while waiting in the doctor's office.

ENTERTAINMENT: When "having fun," ask yourself if you are truly enjoying yourself. Determine whether you are you doing the activity for pleasure or out of habit. I have a friend who constantly complains about his Sunday golf outing with his "friends." He has been playing golf every Sunday with the same foursome for many years. It no longer brings him joy, it's a habit that he hasn't examined closely and tried to break. How many things do we do that we tell ourselves are recreational and yet they are more obligatory? This woman's insight beautifully describes the problem: "It's amazing that I have not given thought to rewarding myself before. The usual 'reward' I give myself is something I really don't want, like having another drink or going out with people whom I have absolutely nothing in common with. These are really punishments. Yet I tell myself they are treats." Develop the awareness to examine the activities that you do for entertainment and if they aren't enjoyable, begin to branch out and try another things that you sense might be enjoyable.

ENVY VERSUS ACCEPTANCE: Envy is one of those feelings that has gotten bad press. I use envy in a positive way to examine my life for feelings of deprivation. If something triggers envy in me, then further examination is required to see if there is something missing in my life that I want and what do I need to do about it.

Kathy and I went several years to visit friends at their summer lake home. It's a beautiful house overlooking a scenic lake. Our friends have saved and worked many years to create the retirement home of their dreams and they feel blessed with their new lifestyle. I am happy for them but I feel no envy. I am not a boater, fisherman or swimmer and I wouldn't be willing to make the sacrifices they made to build their dream house.

I have another friend who lives a very diversified life, travels a lot, is constantly exploring new endeavors and starting new businesses. Whenever I'm around him I pick up on his energy and feelings of excitement and I become restless. I am envious of his lifestyle. I use this feeling to tell myself I need to do more experimentation and to take on more projects.

Beware Of Negative Influences

Keep away from people who try to belittle your ambition. Small people always do that, but the really great make you feel that you too can become great.

Mark Twain

A major predictor of whether we remain stuck or whether we grow and experience life more fully is how well we manage our daily influences. We are susceptible to external influences. Always be vigilant and attempt to gravitate towards positive influences (uplifting reading material, fulfilling experiences and inspirational people) and steer clear, as best you can, of negative influences.

The influence of our personal relationships must be understood and managed. Personal relationships can be a reservoir of negativity that needs to be avoided. Friendships often just happen. We need a better criterion for cultivating and developing friendships than just a shared past (grew up in the same town), a common interest (golfing buddies) or geographical proximity (next door neighbor). We need to be as serious about evaluating candidates for friendship as companies are when hiring new employees; we need a much stricter criterion: Are these people nutritional (good for us) or toxic (bad for us)?

Perhaps you feel you can handle the negativity of

acquaintances that you see infrequently (Al's a good ole boy and we were in the army together. Just because he drinks too much, distrusts everybody and bashes the opposite sex doesn't mean that we can't go to a football game once in a while).

The people you see on a regular basis, the people you routinely socialize with pose a big much bigger risk; negative people re-enforce the wrong beliefs, and can be a major contributing factor to remaining stuck, having a pessimistic outlook and struggling to enjoy life.

It's easier to apply the negativity/toxic rule with a new acquaintance. We have the luxury of being highly selective as to which people we choose for a new friendship or romantic involvement. It's much more difficult to apply this rule to relatives, a spouse, longtime friends and co-workers.

Here are some suggestions on how to handle the harder, more complex cases that often involve loved ones:

1. Develop greater awareness: Just having awareness of how susceptible you are to the negativity of others is a great first step. Once you have awareness, more behavioral choices are available.

    I love my wife dearly, but her worry or fretfulness about things I perceive as trivial can be bothersome to me. Kathy has difficulty being supportive of anything she perceives as a risk. I am judicious as to what I share with her and understand that she cannot give me something she doesn't have. Kathy places a high premium on security and I place a high value on freedom.

    Another common trap that needs to be avoided is habitual complaining about things we have no control over. I do my best to avoid all forms of gripe sessions. You always want to focus on solutions, not perceived injustices of the past or all that's wrong with society. A victim mentality stifles creativity and undermines self-confidence.

2. Examine the dynamics of the relationship: We all love to fantasize about one stop shopping in which one individual fulfills all our needs. Ask yourself if you are looking for too much out of the relationship. You can't expect someone to give you what he or she is not capable of providing. Perhaps you need to balance this relationship by depending on it less and adding other more positive influences to your life.

3. Understanding reality and being practical: Don't waste energy by trying to help people who aren't willing or ready to be aided. You aren't responsible for that person's life or happiness. Nothing of significance is going to happen until the other person is ready to change. There is the story about the farmer who tried to teach his pigs to dance the polka; it was a complete waste of time and it also agitated the hell of out the pigs.

4. Action always speaks louder than words: Remember that being the best you can be always sends a far stronger message than preaching. People learn from your behavior more than from what you say. Sometimes you have to view this from a long-term perspective. I love my kids (now adults) but I refuse to have an unhealthy relationship with them. Over time our relationships have become less dysfunctional, more honest and are now the best they have ever been.

5. Forgiveness: Try to see the innocence in the other's behavior. Remember that we are all doing the best we can. Try to understand the influences that have conditioned the person to behave in a negative or toxic fashion. It's makes it less painful to be around that person. This quote by Goethe is scotch taped to my bathroom mirror: "Be kind, for everyone you meet is

fighting a hard battle."

6. Set Limits: Control the circumstances and limit the amount of time that you are around a troublesome person. As you become stronger and less influenced by that person's behavior, you can then reconsider spending more time with that individual. The limits only have to be known by you; it isn't necessary for the other person to know. Telling the other person can feel like blame to the person and may have a counterproductive effect on the relationship.

7. Call a time out: Kathy uses this technique. If the relationship isn't working, Kathy will discuss her concerns about the relationship with the person and suggest that they suspend their relationship for a while and get together later and see if they can redefine the relationship in a more healthy way. Usually the other person is also aware that it isn't working and is receptive to Kathy's suggestion.

8. End the relationship: I recently terminated a long-term relationship with someone whom I shared several common interests. Whenever I was with this person I *always* felt either upset, depressed, frustrated or angry. Although it's difficult to end a relationship, you have to act in your best interest.

Never underestimate the impact that relationships have on the quality and enjoyment of your life.

What's Wrong With Always Being Right?

**To be blind is bad, but worse it is
to have eyes and not to see.**

Helen Keller

Can you handle being wrong? The compulsion to be right prevents breakthrough insights, discoveries and other creative possibilities. When you think or *know* you are always right, your awareness is like a flickering light bulb and you have trouble seeing what is happening and have less sensitivity to changing circumstances. These are the times in life that you can really be blindsided. Failure often occurs not because you don't know something, but because you spend time and energy defending a premise that is no longer true or clinging to rules and practices that are irrelevant, outdated and ineffectual. Knowledge and understanding needs to be viewed as dynamic and constantly changing.

Information has a short shelf life. In 10 years, at least 1/4 of all current "knowledge" will be obsolete. In some areas of the computer industry, 1/2 of the knowledge is obsolete in 6 months. Charlie Rose asked a panel of experts what makes highly successful people in the Silicon Valley. The answer wasn't smarts; you can buy that. It was the ability to trust one's intuition and to acknowledge to yourself that you thought you knew something but didn't and immediately change course. Always be evaluating what works and what doesn't and immediately let go of that which doesn't work.

Males seem to have a problem asking for help. Ask any women whose mate refuses to stop and ask for directions. These women might feel great empathy for Rebecca Boone whose husband, Daniel Boone, once said, "I have never been lost, but I was bewildered once for the three days."

Because I have a background in marketing and writing promotional copy, I write all the advertising and descriptive literature for my seminars. I once submitted a class description for a catalogue and without my permission the description was revised. My first thought was "How dare they! Don't they know what a talented writer I am?" The seminar sold out; it was standing room only. Based on that experience, I revised the description that would be published in other catalogues. I was willing to learn and let go of the necessity of being right.

I use to believe that exchanging business cards was a meaningless ritual and a waste of time. I was wrong. What I failed to realize was that though it may be a waste of time in certain situations, it's a social convention and not exchanging business cards is like not shaking hands. It's a slight rebuff and is a subtle way of offending people. It never makes sense to needlessly offend people either in a business or a social setting.

If you don't permit yourself to be wrong, you may feel that you are eliminating risk and avoiding mistakes. You aren't. Rain falls equally on the just and the unjust and bad things happen to good people. What you are eliminating is the aliveness and excitement of new adventures. Mistakes are the greatest teachers in life. Churchill said, " If you want to double your rate of success, double your rate of failure." If you aren't making mistakes and you are always right, it simply means that you aren't doing anything new. If you aren't doing anything new, how can you grow? If you aren't growing, how can life be exciting? You are stuck!

People who pride themselves on always being right cease to investigate alternatives or even think about alternatives. Creativity is founded upon the ability to consider alternatives. If you do not allow yourself to constantly ask "what if" questions, you will lead a limited life. A powerful question is "What if I'm wrong?" If you cannot consider that question, you allow yourself no wriggle room in life. Rigidity (mental rigor mortis) sets in and with this limited flexibility, you lose touch with reality and believe that you have greater control over events than really exists. No amount of blindly following rules will eliminate the randomness of life.

The secret to success and growth isn't being always right. Nobody is always right. It's acknowledging and responding to changing circumstances. It's living in the present in which are you constantly evaluating your life and making the necessary daily adjustments to the changing reality. A sailboat can be off course 99% of the time, but it constantly tacks back and forth and arrives at the planned destination. It's not bad decisions that do us in, it the unwillingness to let go of bad decisions. Always be considering your choices and options in life and have the courage to make the necessary adjustments.

If you can never be wrong, you will never allow yourself to be a beginner and that prohibits you from trying new things and pursuing new ventures. This requires unlearning the way you were conditioned in school. In school the emphasis is on being right. We are taught the right way to do things, the correct facts, and the correct deductions to make. So the real lesson we were learning was how to conform, how to obey always and automatically the rules of rightness. When we blindly do what's right, our ability to ask, "Is this the best way?" or "Why are we doing this?" atrophies. We cease to challenge assumptions.

You have probably heard the story of the housewife who would cut off both end of the roast before placing it in a pan for cooking. When asked why, she said that's the way her mother did it. When the mother was asked why, she said that the way her mother cooked roasts. When the grandmother was asked why, she said that her pan wasn't big enough and she had to cut off both ends of the roast to make it fit.

If you think you are always right, you are cheating yourself out of considering possibilities that could add so much meaning and joy to your life.

Christmas
Is It The Joy Of Giving Or
The Depression Of Giving?

**The most exhausting thing in life
is being insincere.**

Anne Morrow Lindberg

It takes courage to be real, to be authentically yourself. I no longer exchange Christmas presents with family or friends. My exception to the rule of non-giving at Christmas is giving gifts to children. They haven't yet been corrupted and it's truly a joyous time for them.

The first time I mentioned this in class, a few people wrote in their notes "Don't give Christmas presents." That's obviously not the point. The point is to have the courage to be yourself and to do what makes sense to you.

My take on giving is that it should be unconditional. Give for the joy of giving and don't expect payment in kind. We all know the problem when Aunt Emma, who you hardly know or remember, gives you that obligatory gift that is so irrelevant to who you are. Irrelevant gifts can only be given by virtual strangers who haven't a clue about what you like or appreciate. Then, of course, you are obligated to send Aunt Emma some equally meaningless gift. Then it escalates into the dilemma of whether to exchange presents with Aunt Emma's kids. Where is all the joy in this? I want the freedom and reserve the right to not only give unconditionally, but spontaneously any day of the year. Why does giving have to occur only on December 25? The purpose of the celebration has been preempted by consumerism and I refuse to be an unwilling participant.

There is so much depression associated with the holiday season. Many people go into needless debt at Christmas time and participate in hollow rituals that fail to bring joy.

Kathy and I try to do only those things that create joy. We stay away from office parties, where compulsory overeating and excessive drinking are the orders of the day. We avoid, like the plague, crowded malls populated by depressed people going through the motions of pretending to have a good time. We listen to Christmas carols, burn candles and celebrate a small, simple joyous Christmas with our loved ones. I'm also freed of the burden of standing in long lines the day after Christmas, exchanging presents that I didn't want in the first place.

Money:
Do You Control It or
Does It Control You?

**If you are going to let your fear of poverty
govern your life your reward will be that you
eat, but you will not live.**

George Bernard Shaw

When I teach *How to Leave The Job You Hate And Find The Life You Love* seminars, money issues seem to dominate the discussion. Often the reason for seeking new employment is that the current job doesn't pay enough. We have two ways to address the "lack of money" issue: either make more or spend less. Financial worries create real stress. When scarcity dominates our thinking, we fail to see solutions to our problems. Running short of money often isn't the real problem. It might be a symptom that indicates lack of creative thinking. Creative thinking enables you to spawn multiple solutions. Consider establishing a "solutions quota" and don't stop until you have filled your quota. This forces you to view your dilemma from different vantage points. Fresh perspectives can generate new, creative solutions.

Whether you take action or merely congratulate yourself for generating original "thinking out of the box" solutions is another issue. You might have discovered a remedy that has merit, but you don't have the awareness to appreciate its potential or the courage to follow up with action.

There is the story of a man in a flood waiting for God to rescue him. The waters had begun to rise and a boat comes by and he is asked whether he wants assistance. He declines. The waters continued to rise and he has to go up to the second floor of his house. Another boat came by offering assistance. He declines. The waters rose even higher and he had to get up on his roof. A helicopter offered to evacuate him to higher ground. He declines. Finally the floodwater rose another eight feet and he was swept away and drowned. When he got to heaven, he asked God why he didn't save him. God responded "What do you mean? I sent help 3 times."

We need to be aware enough and open enough to see and consider all solutions. Here are some examples of what I am talking about:

A lonely person living in a large house who is having trouble making the house payments fails to consider taking in a boarder. A solution that might solve two problems: economics and loneliness. The real issues are the inability to create and consider new ideas and probably a strong resistance to change.

People struggle with large house payments who have never investigated the possibility of refinancing their mortgage at a lower interest rate. They are intelligent people whose inertia prevents them from reducing their financial burdens.

I know someone who bought a very expensive larger new house because she needed additional space. She now sees that space wasn't the real issue, it was more an issue of confronting and dealing with clutter and lack of organization.

Struggling with clutter seems to be a universal problem.

Kathy and I had a lot of stuff that we no longer wanted; most of the items were either candidates for garage sales or donations to Goodwill. We found a better alternative. There is an online auction service called Ebay. You scan in a picture of what you want to sell and the bidding is done over the Internet. We made about $4000.00 in 3 months selling our "clutter." It was a win-win situation. It was fun and profitable!

Many define who they are (identity & self-worth) by their net worth or their position in the corporate pecking order. But what happens if you get laid off or your company shuts down? If your total self-worth is tied to work and career, then who are you? When your self-worth is attached to external circumstances that you have no control over, you are happy when good things happen to you and sad/depressed when bad things happen to you. You become an emotional yo-yo. A healthier stance that produces serenity rather than stress is to understand and accept that no matter how much money, power or influence you have, you win some and you lose some.

We have been conditioned to believe that there is an overly strong correlation between money and happiness. If it were true, then all rich people would be happy and almost all teenagers would be depressed. Kirby Puckett (former Minnesota Twins star baseball player) agonized for 6 months over whether to go to play for another team for 33 million or stay in Minnesota for 30 million. What conceivable difference could the extra 3 million make in terms of life style and happiness? Kent Hrbek (another Twins ballplayer) was confronted with the same issue and understanding that money isn't everything cheerfully elected to remain with the Twins for less money.

Prosperity is a way of living and thinking, not just the possession of money. Poverty is a way of living and thinking, not just the lack of money.

A good question to ask yourself: "Do you have a

healthy relationship with money?" Do a little self-examination and ask yourself the following questions:

A. Do you save part of your income on a regular basis? When you live paycheck to paycheck, you limit your options when unexpected emergencies arise. Your only option may be to add additional debt to your credit card or to sell something quickly. The "paycheck to paycheck" crowd is the market for the pawnshop industry. You also limit your options when unexpected opportunities arise. You have seen the house of your dreams and you know it's a steal but you don't have enough money for a down payment and cannot capitalize on the opportunity. This is one of the reasons the rich get richer and the poor remain poor. The affluent are positioned to move quickly and capitalize on opportunities. The more you save, the more options you have and the less you will be forced into making untimely, bad decisions.

Practice saving a percentage of your income every paycheck. Accumulating wealth is only half the fun. Savings will provide you the opportunity to be a better, more discriminating shopper. It's fun learning to be a good shopper. After developing the discipline to save, you need to learn basic investing principles and consider ways to obtain the best return on your money. If you are a complete rookie when it comes to investing, consider the stock market. I highly recommend the Motley Fools who have published 3 books (*You Have More Than You Think: The Motley Fool's Guide To Investing What You Have, The Motley Fools Investment Guide and The Motley Fools Rule Breakers, Rule Makers: The Foolish Guide*

To Picking Stocks). They also have a great web site. The point they make is that anyone should be able, over the long haul, to realize a return of at least 10.5% on their stock market investments. If you are willing to spend more than an hour a year, you should be able to improve that rate of return. Now combine that knowledge with the theory of compound interest and you are onto the secret of making money the easy way. For instance, if you invested $10,000 dollars @ an annual growth rate of 10.5%, you would have $73,662 in 20 years, $542,614 in 40 years and $3,997,023 in 60 years. The point to be made is you have to develop awareness about the impact that saving and investing will have on the quality of your life. Saving and investing should be part of the curriculum taught to our kids in school. I don't know what should have a higher priority.

B. Do you understand the concept of good debt vs. bad debt? Paying interest on your mortgage is good (you are buying something that will appreciate in value). Paying 18.5% interest on a maxed out credit card is questionable. As you begin to develop greater awareness of what's good debt vs. bad debt, you can examine your patterns of spending and find more ways to use your money more wisely. People feel blessed when they receive a big tax refund. Large tax refunds are really a product of poor planning rather than good fortune. You have paid your taxes prematurely and you are allowing the government free use of your money. A better strategy would be to allow that money to work for you (invest in something that appreciates in value or pays dividends) and pay what you owe at tax time but not before.

C. Do you comparison shop? Train yourself to always ask the price of a service before you buy. Here is an interesting insight into how businesses set prices. Direct mail marketers often publish different prices in different catalogues targeted at different market segments. When you call to order, the sales representative will ask for your customer number or catalog number. This determines the price you will pay. The goal of these pricing maneuvers is to capture the business of price-sensitive shoppers while harvesting a higher profit margin from shoppers who aren't as diligent or concerned about price. Merchants are setting prices according to what individuals are willing to pay.

D. Do you periodically examine your daily expenditures? Are there patterns of unnecessary and routine waste (phone calls from pay phones, ATM charges, parking fees or 6 bucks spent on 3 cups on "designer/yuppie" coffee)?

E. Do you adhere to the "all prices are negotiable" theory? It never hurts to ask: "Is this your best price?" or "Will this be on sale in the future?" What is the worst that can happen? I spend a lot of time in Barnes & Noble and I probably pay less for my coffee and book purchases than you because I was willing to negotiate a better price.

When talking to high school age kids, I try to make the point that becoming wealthy is easier than they think, if they are willing to learn and follow a few simple rules. Any 18-year-old kid can become a millionaire if he saves, learns some simple investment strategies and understands the theory of compound interest. I stress the following three points:

1. You have to adopt a long-term perspective and understand and appreciate the principle of compound interest.

2. You have to make saving and investing a way of life.

3. You have to learn to always live within your means.

If you have trouble living within your means and your salary suddenly doubled you would probably still have trouble living within your means. You have become conditioned to living beyond your means and being in debt. Many extremely wealthy people are very frugal - always living comfortably within their means. This respectful attitude towards money is why they were able to amass wealth.

Learn to live within your income: this is the lesson that must be mastered if you wish to minimize stress (created by financial worries) and maximize wealth.

Don't Worry, Be Happy

The longer we dwell on our misfortunes, the greater is their power to harm us.

Voltaire

In doing counseling and teaching, I encounter people desperately seeking magic words of wisdom to banish their worries and woes forever. Being an "ex-worrier," I have real empathy and would like to share a couple of insights that might lighten the burden.

Focusing on the good things in life reduces the amount of time you will devote to worrying. Emerson said, "A man is what he thinks about all day long". How could we possibly be anything else? The following strategy will help in redirecting your focus:

On a daily basis, record 5 things that you are thankful for. We need to be reminded of the many pleasures of life that we take for granted. You can do this "on the cheap" using a plain pad of yellow legal-size paper. If you would to add a touch of elegance to this ritual, Sarah Ban Breathnach has published a wonderful little workbook called *The Simple Abundance Journal of Gratitude*. Check it out at your local bookstore.

It's really difficult to worry when you are relaxed. When worry begins to win the battle for your serenity, get a massage, take a sauna, walk outside on a beautiful day or go fishing. Do something that you find relaxing. It puts life into proper perspective. Life is meant to be enjoyed, not endured. As Auntie Mame said, "Life is a banquet and most poor fools are starving to death."

My sense of humor sometimes gets me into hot water. I find the following quote by Elbert Hubbard to be useful in forgiving myself and not burdening myself with the worry that I might say something that I find terribly witty, but another person finds offensive: "Every man is a damn fool for at least 10 minutes every day. Wisdom consists in not exceeding that limit." I allow myself much more than 10 minutes each day to do foolish and goofy things. Give yourself permission to be human and make mistakes.

Steven Covey has an excellent visualization exercise in his book *The Seven Habits Of Highly Effective People*. Imagine a large circle - that is your sphere of concern. Then imagine a bull's eye within the large circle - that is your sphere of influence. Focus on the bull's eye.

When you are worrying, you have a bunch of negative thoughts rattling around in your brain and you bounce from one negative thought to another. The next time you begin to worry, write down your worries. Once they are captured and isolated on paper, they lose their potency. You will view your concerns and worries in a much more objective way.

Always keep in mind, the only things in life we really have control over are our perceptions and ourselves. When we quit trying to manage the universe and practice acceptance, life becomes easier and worry diminishes.

Next time you are in a worrisome state, try this exercise:

1. Analyze the situation and determine what is the

worst that could happen.

2. After determining the worst that could happen, reconcile yourself to accepting it (you will begin to feel relaxed and a sense of calm).

3. From that time on, calmly devote your time and energy to improve upon the worst you have already accepted mentally.

Acceptance of what has happened is the first step in overcoming the consequences of one's misfortunes. When we have accepted the worst, we have nothing more to lose.

Ninety percent of the things we worry about never come to pass and the other 10% aren't showstoppers.

Montaigne said, "A man is not hurt so much by what happens, as by his opinion of what happens"

Why Use The Personals?

Each friend represents a world in us, a world possibly not born until they arrive. And it is only by this meeting that a new world is born.

Anais Nin

There seems to be two schools of thought as to the best way to find eligible people willing to develop and nurture a romantic relationship.

Some people are passive and believe that you should just develop your interests, do the things you like to do and sooner or later a person who shares your interests will appear and a relationship will just happen naturally. What will be will be.

Others (like myself) believe that finding a lover is like finding a job. You have to be proactive. Don't just wait for social opportunities to come along, seek them out and maximize the opportunities.

I met my wife through the personals and we both passionately believe it's a wonderful way to meet people. I would like to share with you our reasons for enthusiastically endorsing the use of the personals:

1. They are inexpensive and a cheap way to meet people. Compare the cost to dating services.

2. Composing an ad forces you to search for your positive attributes and makes you get in touch with what you have to offer.

3. It's an alternative to bar hopping and party going; this might be a great option for shy, serious people who feel their better qualities are not appreciated at wild and crazy parties.

4. You will meet people you would have never met otherwise. How many new eligible people do you meet in a month following your regular routine?

5. The personals allow you to plan all aspects of the dating process. This can be an advantage over having to juggle your schedule to make time for unanticipated social functions.

6. When you begin to meet people on a regular basis, you quit trying to make the unworkable work or settling for far less than you desire.

7. You know everyone that you meet is interested in pursuing some sort of a relationship. Have you ever met someone in a grocery store and they ask you where the bananas are and you don't know whether they are interested in bananas or you?

8. It's safe and fun. There used to be a stigma attached to meeting people through the personals (only weird and desperate people used the personals). Today it's socially acceptable.

    Kathy and I dated over 200 people through the personals and never had a bad experience, but always use common sense. If someone sounds unstable during a phone conversation, don't agree to meet him or her. If somebody sounds clinically depressed and is in a lot of pain, they are probably not ready for a relationship. If someone wants to meet you at 4 am in front of a liquor store, that should raise a red flag.

9. If you place an ad you are in control:

   A. You can determine the type of people you meet by the ad that you write.

   B. You can choose which people you want to meet, when and where you want to meet.

10. There is nothing better for your ego than when you receive your first batch of responses from your ad. It's a great feeling.

11. The personals are a great place to brush up and practice your social skills. A writer once said, "All my life, I have suffered from three major fears: death, abandonment and calling men on the telephone".

    It's been my experience that people are genuinely delighted that you have selected their letter or phone message to answer. If calling virtual strangers on the phone is hard for you, the nervousness/terror will go away after several calls and a little practice.

    Kathy and I both agree that the personals were a source of tremendous personal growth in terms of gaining confidence and improving our social skills.

12. Sometimes when there isn't a romantic connection, you might make a friend.

13. Another great advantage is by meeting a lot of different people you can clarify what you are looking for in a mate.

If you don't know where to look for eligible mates and you want to get going right away, you can start today with the personals!

Blame

If your life isn't working don't blame the product. If your everyday life seems poor, don't blame it; blame yourself; admit to yourself that you are not enough of a poet to call forth its riches; because for the creator there is no poverty and no poor indifferent place.
Rainer Maria Rilke

I think blaming has become the national pastime in America. Blame manifests itself in many ways in all aspects of our lives. The boss didn't...; my wife doesn't understand that...; if I could only get a break; it's not my fault that... The list goes on endlessly.

Two simple questions that you need to consider. When you are blaming, how does that make you feel? Blame never, never evokes positive feelings or makes you feel good. You never feel joyous or uplifted after blaming. If you want to be viewed as petty and desire to attract other petty people into your life, continue to make blame a way of life.

The next question: Does it work? Blame never works. The abdication of responsibility never works. Who is responsible for your life and your happiness? You are! It's so easy to blame others; unfortunately it never works.

Occasional venting is normal and healthy. Chronic blaming only guarantees that you will wallow in self-pity and continually reinforces your self-image of being a victim. Victims have found a way to feel bad and undermine the natural joy of living.

Blaming never contributes to a solution. Practice acceptance of reality rather than conjuring up a distorted view of how it should be. Then train yourself to ask empowering questions. After you are satisfied that your perception is accurate and is closely aligned with reality, ask yourself: how would I like to change this and what's a good first step that I can take? Whenever things don't turn out the way you planned, ask yourself, "What can I learn from this?". With practice, empowering questions will replace blame as your initial response to life situations that you desire to transform.

How Do We Get That Way And Why Do We Have These Problems?

Fear less, hope more; eat less, chew more; whine less, breathe more; talk less, say more; hate less, love more; and all good things are yours.

Swedish Proverb

Therapy sessions are usually kicked off with a series of probing questions concerning your childhood, your parents, your parent's beliefs, early school experiences, and your first friends or lack of friends. The therapist wants to understand what is commonly called your family of origin. The revelation of childhood experiences helps explain the patterns of adult behavior.

If you have ever watched a mid-afternoon talk show that features troubled teens, you will immediately understand the family of origin concept. First you are introduced to the teenager and then you meet the parent(s). Frequently a single mom (unmarried or divorced) and living in poverty. You ask yourself how could it be otherwise? Misery begets misery. Low self-esteem begets low self-esteem. Studies have shown that high percentage of rapists were people who were abused as children.

Most of the childhood messages we received were negative or limiting. Children are bombarded with messages like: don't touch that, act your age, quit acting like a child or you are not old enough. One of the first words children learn is no. It's the exceptional parent that says "go ahead dear, take a chance, expand your comfort zone, try something new". By the time we are adults, we have received an incredibly large number of negative and limiting messages. Is it no wonder that most of our current thoughts (estimates run as high as 90%) are negative and create first responses to new situations that are laced with doubt?

Family of origin work helps you develop awareness about the root causes of your issues. Meaningful personal growth is difficult and requires commitment. This realization shouldn't be an excuse not to change, but minimizes the frustration when change isn't as easy as you anticipated.

One of my issues in life is having a cavalier attitude about money and being financially irresponsible. Money management skills are not my long suit; you would not want me as your financial planner. Why do I struggle with this? My father trained thoroughbred racehorses and gambled for a living. He was a colorful, bigger than life, character. When I was about 11, my dad had won $13,000 or, as dad would have said, "made a killing" by betting on one of the horses he trained. A nice chunk of change. Houses could be purchased for that amount in 1950. So my dad, the jockey and I were leaving the racetrack (a small 1/2 mile track located in West Virginia), we were driving along a country road with this big wad of cash resting on the front seat. I was all excited and riding in the backseat. My dad and the jockey were drinking and whooping it up. Suddenly father had a brilliant insight, the kind of thought that only graces your mind after you have consumed a pint of whiskey. They would throw all the one-dollar bills out of the window to reduce the size of the pile and make it more manageable. Luckily we were on a small country road during the evening rather than a major highway during rush hour traffic.

This one incident has been burned indelibly into my brain and characterizes my father's attitude about money. I spent a large part of my youth at the racetrack with my dad; it was quite exciting and exposed me to colorful characters that most novelists can only fantasize about. Dad was my mentor and role model for learning how to manage one's financial affairs.

As a family growing up, we were either "flush" with pockets full on money or flat broke. During the good times it was cash on the barrelhead for whatever we wanted. Dad paid cash for our house and always paid cash when he bought a new car. "Easy come, easy go" was the slogan that dictated our family's lifestyle. "A penny saved is a penny earned" or "Save for a rainy day" were quotes never uttered in our household. Comparison shopping, saving accounts and investing were alien concepts.

How strong was my father's influence? I played high stakes poker as a teenager. I remember, while in high school, borrowing $2000 dollars to bet on one of my father's horses. Of course I bet it all to win. The horse finished second; as a memento of this near miss, I still have the paramutual tickets. My brother was in the airforce and received a large bonus to re-enlist for four additional years of service. While on leave, he lost it all and more in Las Vegas. He begun to write bad checks to cover his gambling debts and eventually had to joined gambler's anonymous. I don't think that it's a coincidence that late in my life I became a commodities trader. Today, I do some day trading and short term investing in the stock market. Having the discipline to practice good money management techniques is the hardest part of stock trading for me. This awareness of my childhood experiences helps me understand and accept why I will probably always struggle with the issue of being financially responsible.

As you begin to understand the influence your early childhood has in shaping your life, you gain greater awareness of why you do the things you do. When my first marriage ended, I had moved out and I was looking for a place to live. I couldn't decide whether to buy or rent, share an apartment or live alone, live in St. Paul or Minneapolis or whether the downtown area would be better for me than the suburbs. I was waffling with indecision; I just didn't know what I wanted and what would be right for me.

A realtor had convinced me to take a look at an apartment she was showing. The moment we drove up, I knew this is where I had to live. I didn't even need to see the apartment or even know or care how much the rent was. I only knew this was it and where I needed to be. The building was a beautiful old brownstone built in the late 19th century.

Why this compelling attraction? When I was a child, I lived with my mom at my grandmother's house in South Carolina. It was a beautiful old southern mansion with large white columns and a huge wrap around porch, most of the 26 rooms had fireplaces with marble imported from Italy. Imagine Tara Hall from Gone With The Wind, and then visualize a house larger and even more beautiful. This was the setting for some of my warmest and fondest childhood memories. The family wealth had since long disappeared and all that was left was this beautiful old house. For a child, it was like living in your own Disneyland, there was so much to explore and enjoy. I loved my grandmother and this house. Old houses provide me with warm feelings and a sense of being nurtured. That was the attraction.

Divorces are traumatic and I needed a nurturing environment where I could put my life back together and begin to heal. I never had realized how influential this childhood experience continued to be in my life. Then I realized it was also no accident that the last house I had purchased during my first marriage was also built in the 19th century and had that familiar ambiance (hardwood floors, stain glass windows, a beautiful staircase) that felt like home to me.

Family of origin work helps you identify the childhood experiences that contribute heavily to defining who you are today and how you are living your life.

Remembering The Past

**Our past is not our potential. Whatever you
may think about yourself, and however long
you may have thought it, you are not just you.
You are a seed, a silent promise.**
Marilyn Ferguson

Many therapists emphasize to the need to get in touch
with your past and possibly relive or experience the pain so
that you can understand it, feel it and let it go. I believe in the
validity of exploring your childhood and understanding the
connection and the shadow it casts over your life today. I
also think this therapeutic approach needs to be balanced
with some cautionary notes.

Understanding my past and its strong influence helps
me accept why personal growth in some areas is easy for me
and other areas is a real struggle that requires a lot of work to
make progress and lasting change.

Memory is selective and we have a bias towards the
negative. In counseling, the focus is on what was wrong in
your past and little acknowledgment about what might have
been right. If you are in counseling, you must have a
problem and if you have a problem, there must be a cause.
So what better culprit than your past. If your past was good
and your parents provided a loving home and support and
you are experiencing problems in your current life and you

can't blame your parents, then the uncomfortable thought might surface that you have to take personal responsibility for your current mess. After all, you are an adult and no longer a child.

I remember once when Kathy and I were receiving marriage counseling and I fell into the trap of recalling only the painful memories of my childhood. The counselor wanted to understand our pasts so he could identify what emotional baggage we might be bringing into the marriage and better understand the dynamics of our relationship. So I launched off into a dissertation of every negative aspect of my childhood I could think of: born with congenital defects (harelip, cleft palate and protruding lower jaw); parents were both alcoholics; grandmother (who lived with us) was crazy as a loon; had to walk to and from school and it was uphill both ways. On and on and on I droned; I sounded like the king in the Broadway musical *The King And I* who would end every sentence with etc., etc., etc. The counselor gasped and remarked that it amazing that I, someone who had suffered that much mental anguish, hadn't been institutionalized.

Everything I had said was true but it didn't tell the whole story and it wasn't balanced by the good experiences in my childhood. Consequently these errors of omission would lead one to draw false conclusions about my childhood. It's too easy to characterize my parents as alcoholics. That's a too simplistic label to apply. My dad would never win any parenting awards, but he was a kind, generous, gentle man who suffered from alcoholism. He loved me as best he could and never showed violence towards me. He provided us with a comfortable middle class existence. My mother also had a drinking problem, but was highly creative and loved by many. Grandmother was a different story. She really was crazy and at times dangerous. She ultimately had to be institutionalized. But grandmother's illness really wasn't that big of burden; it was like having a dog that bites. You just had to be careful around her. It wasn't overwhelming or did we feel our lives were fraught with danger. We all learned how to deal with and manage my grandmother. It's too easy to paint a bleak childhood picture and blame your childhood for all your problems. It's not in your best interest. It's never in your best interest to allow yourself to feel like a victim. Obsessive focus on the shortcomings of your childhood isn't a healthy exercise. My childhood wasn't traditional or perfect, but it certainly was an interesting one. I have fond memories of being raised around horses and traveling with my dad up and down the East Coast to various racetracks. I learned self-reliance at an early age and that's not all bad.

We always have a choice and I think it's in your best interest to focus on what was right rather than forever dwell on what was wrong with your childhood.

The Portable Therapist

Habits are first cobwebs, then cables.

Spanish Proverb

I'm a big believer that you can never get enough inspiration or positive strokes. Our home is adorned with affirmations and positive (sometimes witty) sayings. After my wife complained that she couldn't put her make-up on in the morning, I reluctantly removed all the words of wisdom that were scotch taped to the mirror and placed my "daily doses of inspiration" on a self sticking corkboard mounted on the inside on the bathroom door. Good decorum? No. (Would Martha Stewart approve?) Convenient? Yes. So the question is, what do you do for emotional support when you venture out of the home? Why, you take it with you, silly.

My wallet is crammed full of wisdom calculated to encourage and motivate. My philosophy "do what you love and the money will follow" gives me the luxury of ample space to store inspirational stuff in my wallet. When I had a real job (defined as dutifully doing something I despised for 40 hours a week), this space was occupied by unsightly dirty old ten and twenty dollar bills. No more financial clutter for me. I jest- pursuing your dreams not only leads to a more joyful life, it's the source of energy for achievement and accomplishment. Wealth is often a byproduct of passion. I consider this "stuff" my traveling support system, as Karl Malden said in his credit card ad "Don't leave home without it." Here are a couple of things you would find in my wallet:

Personal mission statement. Corporations have mission statements; why can't individuals? It helps you to focus and will constantly remind you what's really important. Steven Covey in *The Seven Habits Of Highly Effective People* tells you all you need to know to develop a good personal mission statement. Here's mine:

I love Kathy and am truly blessed that she is in my life and will work on giving her the love that she so richly deserves.

I will be there for my kids and accept and love them unconditionally.

I will live each day with courage and a belief in myself. I will remember that to truly live, I must climb the mountain today. This requires creativity, courage, planning and goals. I will trust my dreams and be the prisoner of nothing. I will show love rather than expect love.

My life really began to soar when I learned how to manage and control fear. If you don't learn to confront and work through your fears, you will lead a life of chronic dissatisfaction and never experience all that life has to offer. Susan Jeffer's in her book *Feel The Fear And Do It Anyway* made several profound observations about fear. They changed my life and whenever I feel fear might inhibit my personal growth, I reread these insights:

1. The fear will never go away as long as I continue to grow.

2. The only way to get rid of the fear of doing something is to go out and do it.

3. The only way to feel better about myself is to go out and do it.

4. Not only am I going to experience fear whenever I'm on unfamiliar ground, but so is everyone else.

5. Pushing through fear is less frightening than living with the underlying fear that comes from a feeling of helplessness.

Sometimes when I'm cleaning out my wallet or pulling out my driver's license for ID purposes, I will run across some forgotten bits of inspiration I've stored in my wallet. They are like old friends. I'm always glad to see them.

Tips From A Pro:
How A Librarian Finds Good Books And More Time To Read

No furniture is so charming as books ... even if you never open them or read a single word; the plainest row of books is more significant of refinement than the most elaborately carved etagere or sideboard.

Sidney Smith

Being married to a librarian is a great perk for one who loves to read. I'm a democrat but President Bush said one thing that I'm in total agreement with: "Marrying a librarian was the best decision I ever made." Here are some tips I have picked up from my reading mentor that might help you get more enjoyment out of reading and provide you additional sources for good books:

Establish the habit of always carrying a good book with you and train yourself to take advantage of idle minutes (e.g., waiting in the doctor's office or when a friend is late for a luncheon get together).

Have plenty of good reading material available and always have a "read in progress." When you are in the middle of a good book, you will look forward to having those opportunities to read 5-10 pages.

Create a good home reading environment with a

comfortable chair and good lighting such as a floor lamp that provides plenty of light and can be easily positioned for your reading needs. If noise easily distracts you, buy some earplugs.

If you enjoy biographies, but have trouble wading through the endless minutia of detail contained in a 700-800 page biography, try a juvenile non-fiction book. Many are well written and you can capture the essence and significant facts in a quarter of the time.

If you are experiencing reader burnout, create a "favorite book list" by asking all of your friends to recommend their favorite book. It will help you become less one-dimensional and will expose you to some new reading experiences.

Review the American Library Association's Notable Booklist; it lists all outstanding books published each year and is available at your local library.

Reading more than one book at a time will give you more options. If you have had a rough day at the office, you might prefer light reading to something that is going to require heavy concentration and contemplation.

Commit to reading 25 pages a day.

Keep a journal of good books read. It will give you a feeling of accomplishment and will reinforce your desire to continue your reading program.

Ask a librarian to recommend a book. That's their job!

Inspiration

**We act as though comfort and luxury were the
chief requirements of life, when all that we
need to make us really happy is something to be
enthusiastic about.**

Charles Kingsley

We have all been inspired by an emotional speech, a
well-written book or some example of courage. It's like a
shot of emotional adrenaline; it makes us feel good but it's
short-lived and wears off.

If inspiration is meaningful and makes us feel good, why
do we allow it to only randomly enter our lives? Why aren't
we proactive and seek as much inspiration our psyche can
absorb? If we are products of our environment, why not
make that environment a nurturing environment ladled with
inspirational goodies that make us feel good and motivate us
to grow?

You truly can't afford the luxury of a negative thought.
Eliminate the negativity from your life. Negative thinking is
viewed as reality. Says who? Positive thought is the origina-
tor and foundation for all goods things in life.

Do What You Love

Regret for the things we did can be tempered by time; it is regret for the things we did not do that is inconsolable.

Sydney J. Harris

Every person is born with a life purpose. You will become aware of it if you permit yourself to entertain the thought of making your dreams a reality. How do you discover your purpose in life? Your purpose in life is connected to your passions. What do you love to do? Energy is always available for the things you love to do. You can be bone tired, but if you love to read mysteries, you will stay awake half the night reading that mystery to discover "who done it." People who have lively purpose in their existence are always doing what they want to do.

One of the real secrets to enjoyment and fulfillment isn't to do what you are necessarily good at but to do what you love. It also follows that if you persist in doing what you love you will become more proficient. The saddest specter is to have lived and never had the courage and confidence to pursue your dreams.

The happiest people I know are the ones pursuing their dreams. How about the financial aspect of pursuing dreams? Fortunes are usually a byproduct of someone pursuing their dreams. When you focus on your dreams good things will happen. You have all the necessary resources within you to fulfill your dreams.

Doing what you love requires that you believe in yourself. Total commitment will become a joy and not a burden. People with good self esteem don't ask if; they ask how, because they believe in themselves. This isn't delusional thinking or a false belief. We are all capable of achieving wonderful and joyous things. It isn't a lack of talent that blocks us; it's the lack of a winning attitude. You can never outperform your self-image, which is based on self-esteem. How do you view yourself? We are able to see the potential in others but oftentimes we are blind to our own potential.

You were put on this earth to be the best you can be, not to limit yourself or let others plan or dictate your life. When you really begin to focus on your dreams, decision making becomes much easier. Your subconscious will help you (if you allow it) to decide what activities, people, etc., support your dreams. The greatest gift you have to offer is to be the best you can be, and how can you do that if you aren't pursuing your dreams?

Detachment

> **To lead a simple life in reasonable comfort,
> with a minimum of possessions, ranks high
> among the arts of living. It leaves us the time,
> resources, and freedom of mind we need for the
> things that give life value: loving, helping, serv-
> ing, and giving.**
>
> ***Eknath Easwaran***

Detachment is a hard concept to accept. It's paradoxi-
cal, but true that the easiest way to achieve goals and attain
material wealth is to relinquish our attachment to them.
Attachment creates fear and insecurity. Fear limits flexibility
and demands that you travel a certain path in life. Detachment assures freedom, joy, and creativity. Freedom allows
you to take any path you choose; joy provides a higher level
of energy and creativity makes you privy to new options and
choices. Learning to detach yourself from the need of material wealth and luxury assures serenity and security.

Security can never be attained via material wealth. Lasting and eternal security can never be provided from external
sources because we have no control over external sources.

If you heavily invested in the stock market, there is no
guarantee that some unanticipated event will not create
losses in your portfolio. If you are a highly paid model, age
eventually will take its toll and the security of a well paying
job will be gone. If you have that great paying job, there is
no guarantee either a merger or a downturn in the economy

won't make you susceptible to a downsizing in your company. (Been there, done that.)

Security can never be based on material wealth. Real security can only be attained from within and is based on acceptance and gratitude. This doesn't mean you can't enjoy the good things in life. Life is meant to be enjoyed. Live with gratitude for what you have. Focusing on what you don't have and developing a "must have mentality" isn't the formula for either security or happiness.

If you try to achieve security via material wealth, ask yourself: how much is enough? You may discover that there is never enough because real security and happiness can't be based on external things such as money, cars, houses, etc.

There are some very wealthy and very unhappy people who are driven to acquire even greater wealth. These affluent, unhappy people labor under a very rigid, false assumption that money is the key to security and happiness. Using greed as a basis for establishing financial goals leaves no room for serenity.

I have nothing against success, but never be willing to pay an exorbitant price in terms of happiness and serenity.

New Careers:
Stressful Or Exciting?

No pessimist has ever discovered the secrets of the stars, or sailed to an uncharted land, or opened a new heaven to the human spirit.

Helen Keller

Career changes can be a primary source for stress or an exciting adventure. Planning and a positive attitude will provide a smoother transition and minimize the fear and perceived risks.

The fortunate are those, willing to overcome their fear, who switch jobs in pursuit of their dreams. The decision to change one's employment can be forced upon us. We become victims of downsizing; our spouse's job requires us to relocate; a family member has become incapacitated and we feel responsible for their well-being; health concerns (or just being tired of Minnesota's long winters) force you to relocate to a warmer climate; your present job has become so intolerable that you feel have to leave, or retirement necessitates that you find another source of income to make ends meet.

Sometimes the choice isn't obvious, your company offers you an attractive early retirement package and you aren't sure what to do.

Reality has to be acknowledged by   assessing your

existing financial situation. Do a simple financial projection to determine how long your funds will last. If you can't pay next month's rent, you will have to focus on securing immediate income to keep body and soul together. Job satisfaction will have to be put on the back burner. If your financial situation allows you 12 months or so to make the transition to a new career, you have many more options. The elimination of vagueness pertaining to your finances reduces needless worry. You know exactly where you stand and can plan accordingly.

Good support systems are always important when a major change occurs in your life. A mentor or coach can help you devise strategies to get you from where you are to where you want to be. Two heads are better than one; why reinvent the wheel if you can find someone who has been through the process and can assist you. The mentor can provide continuing support and the necessary accountability to keep you on track. Being unemployed or "between engagements" batters your self-esteem and you might find yourself susceptible to depression. Supportive people can help you cope with your emotions and give you the necessary encouragement to effectively pursue a new job.

The more you know about yourself (values, style, habits, preferences) the greater the probability you will find a job or career that matches your temperament.

Are you a fearless risk-taker or are you more cautious and prudent? Examine your work history. Have you had multiple jobs in different fields and moved around a bit or have you had the same job for 20 years? If you are a risk taker, you might proceed at a faster rate but you won't always be on target. Risk takers have to guard against being impulsive. You need to strive for prudent and measured risk taking that allows you to achieve an acceptable balance in the risk vs. reward equation.

If you are a security oriented person, change might be harder for you and you will need a more detailed plan with all the questions answered. You will also be more comfortable proceeding at a slower and steadier pace.

What's your style or method to get things accomplished? Do you commit to a deadline and then figure out how to do it or do you develop a plan and work your plan? What motivates you? People, books, ideas, opportunities, dreams of power and prestige, a nurturing environment?

If you are stuck in a dead end job or underemployed and have delayed looking for other employment opportunities, you need to examine the reasons for your procrastination. One of the main reasons for this resistance to change could be fear. Fear that will you fail, fear of success in that growth or good fortune might alienate you from family members or other loved ones, an unconscious fear that you might do better than your father, fear that success will make you greedy or force you to violate your values. Awareness as to where you are limited by fears is the first step in controlling your fears.

If you are making a radical change that frightens you or that you perceive as a high risk situation (e.g. leaving the security of a well paying job with benefits to strike out on your own), get some questions answered before you commit yourself beyond the point of no return. Suppose you feel that you will have to moonlight and take a part time job to supplement your income while waiting for your business venture to grow and become profitable. Consider taking a part time job *before* you leave your current job to test how well you handle working two jobs and whether you ego suffers too much from the reduced status of a part time job. It's better to discover undetected flaws in you plan while you have options. If the test is successful and you can handle working two jobs, you will have eliminated an area of doubt and will have more confidence in the success of your new venture.

People have a tendency to do the easier, fun things first when going into business for themselves. Office furniture will be ordered, new computers will be installed and a lifetime supply of expensive business cards will be purchased. It's always easier to spend money than to make money. After making these expensive purchases, they might discover that there is no market for their products. I would suggest test marketing your product or service by generating some sales and establish a small customer base, before spending money on non-revenue-generating items.

Another requirement for the new entrepreneur is to make sure he fully understands the essence and all the features of starting up a new business. It's easy to identify with the freedom of being your own boss, working your own hours aspect of self-employment. There are other less glamorous features. The responsibility of wearing multiple hats. You no longer submit your drafts to your secretary or the typing pool; *you are the secretary*. The absence of clerical support is often overlooked or erroneously minimized. You might have been good at your corporate job, but new skills may be needed. Do you have experience in marketing and sales? Are you comfortable being a shameless promoter of your new venture?

There is no longer the camaraderie of the office; isolation can be a problem. Dixie Darr, publisher of the *Accidental Entrepreneur*, says there are 4 warning signs that it's time to get out of the house:

1. You realize it's been 3 days since you talked to anyone but your cat.

2. You get upset if the mailman is late delivering your mail.

3. When you go to the library or Post Office you're *really* friendly to the clerks.

4. You become a regular caller on talk radio.

The self-employed have to set their own business objectives and deadlines. You will have to fight the tendency to turn on the television or do household chores or make another pot of coffee rather than buckling down to work.

How committed are you to your venture and what sacrifices are you willing to make? If you have doubts or reservations, commit to making $100 before reassessing your situation. This simple small commitment will ensure that you progress beyond the conceptual or wishful thinking stage and have transitioned from thinking to doing.

A good resume and cover letter are essential to the job search in the corporate world. The purpose of the resume isn't to "make the sale" or get the job, but to pique the employer's interest and to get you an interview. The interview is where you have to convince the employer that you are the right candidate for the job. These two books are worth reading if you want a dynamite resume that works!

The Damn Good Resume Guide - Yana Parker

The Overnight Resume - Donald Asher

Two other books that would be invaluable to corporate job seekers are:

Knock Em' Dead "Great Answers To Tough Interview Questions" - Martin John Yates

Overnight Job Change Strategy - Donald Asher

Networking is an effective way to advertise and to market. It's important to target the right people in the right industries. Don't fall into the trap of networking with other networkers who really aren't in a position to help you advance towards your career goals. Smart people make use of all their networking resources: family, social contacts and friends.

When you do research to find the ideal job or vocation, informational interviews can be useful. Contact people in the appropriate field or industry and explain your interest and goals; ask them if would they be willing to grant a 20-minute interview. This is for information gathering purposes only. Do not abuse the privilege by seeking employment.

New Careers can be an exciting adventure. Have confidence in yourself and everything will turn out for the best.

190

The Second Time Around

Every one who knows how to read has it in their power to magnify themself, to multiply the ways in which they exist, to make life full, significant and interesting.

Aldous Huxley

I reread two books by Deepak Chopra (The *Seven Spiritual Laws of Success: A Practical Guide to the Fulfillment of Your Dreams* and *The Way of the Wizard: Twenty Spiritual Lessons for Creating the Life You Want*). I was surprised by how much more I got out of the books the second time around. The first time I read the books, I mentally classified them as new age hokum with little practical value. At that time, I unknowingly wanted "how to" books that would provide simplistic, formulaic solutions to my problems. If life were only that easy.

It intrigued me why something would hold so much more meaning for me when read the second time. I concluded the following:

1. I'm a different person today (older and hopefully a little wiser) than I was when I first read these books.

2. I think I suffered from the expectation that if I read enough self-help books, I would find one that had

all the answers and my problems would be resolved. (One of my issues in life is that I'm always looking for the easy solution and I'm reluctant to pay the necessary dues required to achieve mastery or understanding.) I wanted to believe that I then would live happily and blissfully ever afterwards. My current view is that if a book contains a glimmer of some new truth or helps me to clarify, hone or refine some previous belief or insight, the book has been a successful read.

3. I think Deepak Chopra's books contain a lot of wisdom and I don't doubt his sincerity or motives for writing the books. I also think that some of his beliefs and philosophy fall into the category of advanced study or self help 107. It's necessary to do a lot of prerequisite work before fully understanding the essence of what he has to say. It's like taking 5th year French without bothering to take the beginning or intermediate courses - you feel lost.

From a personal perspective, I think that there is some benefit to this approach; it makes you stretch and grow. If everything you are reading consists of concepts that you already know and understand, then all you are doing is rattling around in your comfort zone. Knowing that we have this tendency to stick with what we comfortably know, I purposely read books that make me think, "what the hell is this all about?"

From a spiritual perspective, I'm find real meaning in many of the eastern philosophies, especially Buddhism. When I try the read the literal or original text, I'm lost. I have to have a knowledgeable interpreter. The wisdom is there, but it's so hard to overcome the cultural barriers. Reading 500 BC eastern thoughts with 20th century western eyes is a daunting task. Another example of a difficult (but worthwhile) read is *A Course Of Miracles*. I would recommend cutting your teeth on Mary Ann Williamson's *A Return To Love*, before tackling *A Course Of Miracles*.

4. I had to overcome the belief that you shouldn't read a book a second time, until you have read all the good ones a first time. Rereading seemed like a waste of my finite time and energy. Now I will often quickly scan or speed-read a book to decide whether it's worth reading in depth. If I choose to read the book, I will have developed a frame of reference or outline in which to place the detailed knowledge. This pre-established framework allows me to retain a lasting and much more thorough and comprehensive understanding of the subject matter.

5. A good reporter always collaborates his facts and story from several sources. I think the same principal applies to self-help concepts or insights. When I discover the same concepts independently arrived at by several authors, I pay heed and say to myself there might be something here that's valid and worth knowing. Meditation was a concept that never grabbed my attention in a serious way, however many people whose books and thinking I respected were extolling the virtues of meditation. I now get it and make it part of my daily program. Five or ten minute of meditation in the afternoon relaxes and rejuvenates me. Meditation helps to reduce the mental chatter and quiet the mind.

6. In the spirit of truthful advertising, I think self-help books should contain a proviso in the front that says the following concepts and strategies are

sound, but that no one including the guru that wrote the book has thoroughly mastered them. We are led to believe that if you practice what the author preaches, the path will be easy. Very few writers admit that personal growth and mastery of anything is a lifelong quest of uneven progress consisting of breakthrough insights and occasional relapses.

If you were to read Deepak Chopra's book you would be led to believe that here is a person who has attained perpetual serenity and bliss. I once saw him get highly agitated on a television show over something that seemed relatively trivial.

A prominent eastern mystic, who is widely quoted and revered by students for his spiritual practices, died of alcoholism. (Nobody ever mentions or footnotes this.)

I have been doing some research on present moment living and consciousness raising techniques. Living in the present is a very simple concept to explain and even understand, but it's hard to practice! After reading numerous books and suffering an increasing level of frustration in not being able to practice, I want to preach. I ran across a quote by Charles Tart (a leading authority on consciousness-raising techniques) who indicated that the best we can hope to achieve each day would be measured in minutes rather than hours. Our minds keep wanting to dwell in the past or jump to the future.

A question that I've recently gotten answered is what's wrong with a good fantasy. The answer is nothing is wrong with a good fantasy. Present moment living and fantasies are mutually exclusive concepts. The trick is to have control over when you are fantasying and when you are living in the present. Fantasies or daydreaming could be dangerous while driving a racecar or performing brain surgery, but would be ok when sitting in your easy chair at home. The risk associated with excessive fantasizing is that you reinforce the habit of day-dreaming about what you want instead of pursuing what you want. An imagined life pales in comparison to a fully lived life.

Currently not only am I rereading books, but I'm can be talked into seeing a good movie a second time. I delight in discovering nuances and gaining better understanding made available by a second effort.

Procrastination

**Procrastination is thinking the moment is to-
morrow. It is not a way to let in vital energy.
Procrastination diminishes.**

Natalie Goldberg

My wife, Kathy, is the most productive person I know. Her full life is the envy of her friends. She isn't a workaholic. She works hard and plays hard. A major secret to her success in leading a full life is having the discipline to do what needs to be done and doing it in a timely manner. Procrastination is like a whimpering puppy that has been beaten into submission; it doesn't dare show up and disrupt Kathy's life. Procrastination is like beating your head against the wall; it feels so good when you stop. Kathy was kind enough to contribute this essay on her methods for dealing with procrastination.

Procrastination is the thief of time. That thought never leaves my mind, because it is so true. I value my time in a way that almost drives my husband crazy. I have lists of what I must accomplish every day of my life. They are not lists I compiled years ago; they are fresh lists, made that week or the day before.

Thank you notes? I write them the day I get a present and put them in the mail. Once they are on paper and in the mail, they can get out of my brain, where they take up way too much space. When we hosted a wedding reception brunch to celebrate our marriage, I wrote thank you notes that evening and mailed them out the next day. I mail out my Christmas packet (a customized envelope, Christmas card and a personalized letter) on December 1st. This really lightens the load for an already heavily burdened month. An added bonus is the wonderful, warm replies I receive to my Christmas letters.

Anytime I put off doing something that I have to do, it hangs over my head like a threatening cloud. My life works better and my stress level sinks the minute I start doing whatever it is that must be done.

Do what you have to do
whether you like it or not.

The moment I actually start doing something that has been hanging over my head, it almost always turns out to be not nearly as big of a project as I had feared it would. Well begun is half done. Sometimes when I start something I have been putting off, I am amazed that accomplishing the whole dreaded task may be a ten or fifteen minute operation. But not starting it takes so much time and energy. It is always there, in the back of my mind, waiting.

When I procrastinate, my self-esteem probably suffers more than any other part of me. I don't think much of people who don't do what they said they would do, or don't tell me thank you when I do something special for them, or are just plain careless and irresponsible, letting others pick up the pieces they have dropped. I try very hard to be fair in my life. People who procrastinate aren't fair. Most of the time when we procrastinate, we put off doing something that other people are depending on us to do. Other times, we are not being fair to ourselves.

Making lists helps a lot, and I feel a great surge of satisfaction when I cross something off. I love "to do" note pads, and carry an organizer than has an ample amount of space for those lists.

By focusing on the benefits of doing tasks on time and not focusing on the alleged downside (hey, I could be watching more television!), I find that everything in my life works much better. I am renowned among my friends for "getting more things done than anyone else they know." And the reason I do get so much done is that I do what I have to do. Time is my ally, not my enemy. When I take off to go to the movies, I don't have that nagging, rotten feeling in the back of my brain that "I should be doing such and such." I am free to relax and enjoy myself, because I have done my tasks for the day.

Kathleen Baxter

Hidden Beliefs

> We must be willing to get rid of the life we've
> planned, so as to have the life that is waiting for
> us.
>
> *Joseph Campbell*

Awareness has to precede change. How can we change that which we have no awareness of? We can identify many of our beliefs and make a call as to whether these beliefs are good or bad. We then have the option to eliminate or modify disempowering beliefs that cripple and limit our potential. Unfortunately it's the hidden, undetected beliefs that control our lives. Beliefs that lurk below the level of consciousness rob us of the opportunity for change and choice. Greater awareness provides you more opportunities and freedom.

Sometimes we fail to properly examine or challenge our beliefs and labor under the illusion that they are empowering. We've heard that hard work guarantees success. It sounds good but I don't think it's true. All hard work guarantees is that you have worked hard and nothing more. No guarantees necessarily flow from hard work. Jobs are lost from mergers and unanticipated corporate hard times. Laid off employees can feel victimized and their rebuttal might be "but I worked hard" or " I never took a day of sick leave."

That may be true but perhaps if they had had greater awareness they might have seen it coming and could have better prepared for it. Others might have known it was it was coming, but didn't want to face reality. I think hard work by itself can be highly overrated. When Bobby Kennedy was campaigning for the democratic presidential nomination, a coal worker confronted him with the statement that he understood that Bobby had never worked a day in his life and then said "Believe me, you haven't missed a thing!" Now if you combine hard work with other ingredients - confidence, creativity, awareness of opportunities and risk taking skills, then you have a formula for success.

Some believe that busyness creates self-worth. I believe a life without quiet time for self-reflection and some form of adequate relaxation or play guarantees a limited life regardless of how busy you are.

An often unquestioned belief is that a conventional, full-time, 9 to 5 job is required to make ends meet and survive financially. How do you know that's true? Possibly you could construct a life style consisting of part time jobs (short term gigs often command a higher hourly rate) that would provide stimulating experiences, a wider range of social and business contacts and the opportunity to create ongoing multiple revenue streams.

Creative people can fall prey to believing that if you follow your passions you will be forced to live a meager existence, always scrambling to make ends meet. They have bought into the starving artist syndrome. I think the opposite is true because when you truly follow your passions you have more energy, happiness, purpose, creativity and excitement in your life. How can you accomplish anything really worthwhile or significant without those forces being unleashed?

If you stay perpetually broke and aren't making progress towards your financial goals, perhaps it's because you believe in scarcity rather than abundance (another one of those hidden beliefs). You are choosing to stay stuck by not confronting fears that need to be addressed or stepping outside your comfort zone and doing what needs to be done. Is your resume current or do you even have a resume? When is the last time you have responded to an ad in the paper or have gone on a job interview? If you were willing to relocate, would there be better opportunities for you? Are there opportunities within the company? (Often jobs are posted internally before people are recruited from outside the company.) Have you considered a part time job? Are there ways to enhance your skills so that you are eligible for a better paying position? Have you ever investigated opportunities at a job fair? When is the last time you took a class that would help further your career goals? Are there ways that you could reduce your monthly living expenses? Is there clutter in your existence that could be sold on Ebay (an on-line auction site)? One man's junk may be another's prize possessions. Whenever problems aren't being solved or answers forthcoming, your creativity is blocked.

We get deluded into thinking that if our material wealth is diminished, we will be miserable. How do you know that's true? How do you know that you wouldn't be happier with less - a smaller house, fewer obligations, a simpler lifestyle, an old car that will never be stolen or create worries about someone vandalizing or opening a car door into it? Having less might mean more freedom. If you didn't own a car, you would never have to look for parking spaces in crowded downtown areas or have to experience the pain of what you feel is an outrageous car repair bill. If you lost that prestigious vice presidency, you might not feel as obligated to present a false image or appearance that has to be maintained because of your high profile well-paying job. You might not feel obligated to live in a neighborhood that requires extravagant spending and ruinous debt just to keep up with the Jones. What price does success demand? Are you locked into a job or career that isn't fulfilling and way too stressful?

Does that job require a lifestyle that constantly batters your physical and emotional health? Are you sure that the new expensive carpeting that you covet is going to add happiness to your life? Remember you never got terribly upset when your beloved family pet (a long hair cat) regurgitated a hairball or one of the kids spilt a glass of milk on the old carpeting. Perhaps the accumulating of wealth is the key to misery rather than happiness.

I am writing while comfortably ensconced in my favorite office (the local Barnes & Noble bookstore), and an elderly gentleman plops down beside me with a book entitled *The Healthy Liver And Bowel.* I wonder if his beliefs have allowed him to live a full, conscious and joyful existence. I wonder what beliefs snared him in their trap and didn't allow him to live life day by day and enjoy the experience. Regardless of how much wealth we gather or how strenuously we pursue traditional success, there will come a time when we all might contemplate buying a book titled *The Healthy Bowel And Liver.*

Life is a trip that doesn't need to be burdened with disempowering beliefs. Always be examining and evaluating your beliefs.

On Fear Of Failure

A life spent in making mistakes is not only
more honorable, but more useful than a life
spent in doing nothing.

George Bernard Shaw

We have to learn to develop a healthy relationship with
failure and understand that failure is part of the process of
becoming successful. If we don't forgive ourselves and let go
of our failures, we remain stuck and paralyzed by inaction.

Failure provides necessary lessons required for mastery.
I am not sure that there is a better teacher than failure. We
must be willing to write that bad novel, to have a speculative
investment lose money and to fail at our early en-
trepreneurial attempts. Most wildly successful people have
experienced frequent and large failures before achieving
success. If you haven't experienced any failures, you aren't
experimenting and risking. Undertaking any new adventure
involves an element of risk.

If you cannot learn to accept failure as part of the
process of growth then you run the risk of labeling yourself
a failure and that label becomes a self-fulfilling prophesy.
That label leads you to believing that you have nothing to
offer and no contribution to make. It just simply isn't true;
we all are unique and have gifts to share with the world. Life

is about experimenting and learning how best to share that gift. Don't let fear of failure hold you back from living life fully. As Winston Churchill said "Success is going from failure to failure with no loss of enthusiasm".

Duty Or Delight?

An adventure is only an inconvenience
rightly considered. An inconvenience
is only an adventure wrongly considered.

G. K. Chesterton

If I were to tell you that I'm going to Florence, Italy in two months, you might say to yourself, "That lucky stiff, I wish I could travel and go to exotic, far away and exciting places." If I were to say to you excitedly that I washed dishes last night, your first response would probably be "Huh?" or "I'm paying good money to hear this moron talk?" Let's examine the two experiences.

Take a close look at some of the experiences related to taking a vacation: waiting in an overcrowded airports for flights that might be late or cancelled; snacking (out of boredom) unhealthy and outrageously priced food; traveling long distances in a confined space; eating mediocre meals with microscopic portions; we don't even need to dignify the airplane bathroom experience by discussing it; having thoughts that the plane is attempting to defy gravity in an unnatural way; wondering if those disgruntled mechanics who recently ended a long and bitter strike really have a good attitude and properly tightened all those bolts on the wing; arriving at a foreign airport and having to morph into a pack animal and haul way too much luggage while trying to figure out how to hail a cab or obtain some other form of transportation to your hotel (remember you don't speak the language); remembering it's lunch time and having to screw up the courage and try ordering food from someone who doesn't speak English and might not be particularly fond of Americans and is unwilling or can't translate the menu for you; feeling adventuresome and ordering something off the menu that you've never heard of and discovering the next day that you can't risk ever being further than 15 paces from a toilet; enjoying the experience of paying the bill that requires you to partially disrobe to get at your neck wallet (this is to thwart the ever present pickpockets) and hassling with foreign currency (is it 10,000 lira or 100,000 lira to the dollar?) and saying to yourself "Oh well, never mind we are on vacation; we will just leave about 3 pounds of money that should do it;" arriving at the hotel and getting the key for your postage stamp size room and discovering that your room doesn't have a private bath (the communal bathroom and shower are at the end of the hall); waking up in the morning and learning that your hair dryer or your electric shaver won't work without a special adapter. This is called a vacation.

Now the second experience: The meal has ended; your wife has knocked herself out preparing a meal fit for royalty and it's great to see your brother and his new wife, who are visiting from the east coast. You volunteer to do the dishes and your brother insists that he help. You wash and he will dry. It's great to have the opportunity for some one-on-one conversation with your brother; it brings back fond memories of when you were kids and did the dishes together. Your wife is appreciative of your willingness to pitch in and help. It feels good to dip your hands into warm soapy water; there is a sense of accomplishment when all the dishes are washed, dried and put away. This is labeled a chore.

What can we learn from the comparison of these two

experiences? Attitude and perspective (positive or negative) greatly enhance or diminish an experience. If you think it's a God-awful experience, you are right. If you view it as an adventure with an open mind and allow yourself to enjoy the process, you will reap the benefits that accrue to those who are fortunate to see the wonder and joy in all facets of living.

Pampering The Senses

When you have only two pennies left in the world, buy a loaf of bread with one, and a lily with the other.

Chinese Proverb

I was going to my Saturday morning men's group. The day was overcast and I was feeling slightly down and lethargic. I was driving my wife's car, which has a CD player that's always loaded with sound tracks from the latest Broadway musicals. While waiting at a stop light, I clicked on the car's sound system and it began blaring out foot stomping music from the Broadway musical *The Full Monty*. Within a minute, my mood changed and my spirits were uplifted.

Sometimes you can't think your way out of a funky mood, but you can jump-start the mood altering process by bombarding your senses with new types of stimulation. Music is a great mood alterer. Doesn't everyone feel better after hearing the Star Spangled Banner? Different music is required to create different moods or emotions. If I'm writing, there is a certain kind of background music that is very calming and serene and puts me into a contemplative, creative writing state. Other music (anything by John Phillips Sousa) makes me swell with a feeling of pride and enthusiasm and puts me in a mood where I'm are ready to take on the world and do battle with whatever problems may arise.

War is the ultimate stupidity of man. Misguided patriotism and flag waving hysteria has sentenced many a young man to a senseless and premature death. With that said, I am at the mercy of bagpipe music and I know that if had been born in Scotland during the 18th century, I couldn't have resisted proudly marching off to war to do battle with the English and being slaughtered in the process. That's the power of music. A single sound can trigger a torrent of thoughts and sensations that have been previously relegated to the memory's lost and found box. We all have moments when sound takes us back to another time and place.

Whenever I hear church bell's chiming on a Sunday morning, I feel comforted and nurtured. Bells ringing instantly transport me back to my childhood and warm memories of crawling into bed and snuggling with my mom on Sunday morning before we were off to church. Dr. Rene Dubos, a microbiologist, philosopher, and the author of the book *A God Within*, believes there is great value in living within range of the sound of church bells.

The stimulation of other senses can also trigger that time travel experience. The smell of diesel fuel can dredge up memories of wartime experiences for Vietnam veterans.

The secret is to develop awareness and recognize which stimuli trigger pleasant feelings and build them into your daily existence. Why leave how you feel to chance? Heightened awareness will allow you to hear the chirping of a bird that can remind you (this is very important for Minnesotans) that spring is coming (eventually).

I think man's pursuit of beauty is really a quest to stimulate the senses in a positive way. Enjoyment of life can be enhanced by developing awareness of ways to stimulate our senses (smell, taste, hearing, seeing and feeling). Develop awareness of life's little pleasures and be proactive in the pursuit of them.

Also develop awareness of how stimulation of the

senses can also lead to negative consequences. Be aware of how marketing and sales people manipulate you into impulse buying by creating "feel good" states. Salesmen will say, "You really look good in that suit" or "This brand new convertible Corvette is really you; don't you deserve the best?" I'm a very auditory person and I would buy anything from a young, Irish, red-haired lass with that beautiful, lilting Irish brogue.

A realization of the many little ways we can pamper our senses will add immeasurably to the enjoyment of our daily living. What music do you enjoy? What music inspires you? How about giving your sense of smell a treat? Experiment with burning incense, using potpourri or lighting a scented candle. How about your sense of touch? Doesn't everyone enjoy the feel and smell of clean sheets? I have a longhaired calico cat with very soft, silky fur. It's a win-win situation when I stroke her. It brings us both pleasure. When Kathy and I invite our friends over for a Sunday brunch, the house is filled with the pleasant aroma of a home-cooked meal, a pleasure that is missing from the dining out experience.

What little things can you do to enhance the beauty of your living space? We have replaced all of our light switch plates with beautiful hand painted ceramic fixtures.

Here is one for the taste buds. One of Kathy's Internet friends sent her some Cardamom spice. We used the spice to bake some homemade bread for our traditional Christmas meal that we celebrate with some close family friends. Everybody enjoyed this new and different taste sensation.

Ask yourself what are some ways that you can pamper your senses and increase your enjoyment of life.

What Can I Do Differently?

**Destiny is not a matter of chance,
it is a matter of choice.**

William Jennings Bryan

We get stuck in patterns in which we think the same thoughts over and over and these thoughts trigger the same feelings. These repeated feelings lock us into predictable behavior. The first step required to change these repetitious, non-productive patterns is to ask what can you do differently. How can you respond differently and get a different result?

I am forever dieting and battling my weight. Last night at the movies, I had an unplanned box of popcorn. The old pattern was that whenever I deviated from my planned menu of meals for the day, I believed that I had totally failed and would say, "What's the use?" That would be the end of the diet. This was symptomatic of a much larger, consistent pattern in my life: lack of persistence, giving up before reaching my goal.

Now I accept that small setbacks are just part of the process. The next day I'm back eating according to my plan. I've learned to forgive myself and not beat myself up for my very human shortcomings.

Healthy living is one of my goals in life. Whenever I experience a setback, I ask myself, "What can I learn from this experience?" In this example, what could I have done differently so as not to have eaten that box of popcorn? I allow myself to consider all the possibilities. I could eliminate going to the movies when I am trying to lose weight. For a movie lover, that would feel like some form of unnecessary deprivation. A better solution would have been to schedule my meals so that I wouldn't have been hungry during the movies. If plan A fails, plan B could be to have a low-calorie, healthy snack available if hunger struck.

I am a very introverted person and always run the risk of unhealthy isolation. When Kathy is in town, most of my socialization involves Kathy and is planned around her busy schedule. We go to the movies together, visit her mom weekly and watch Masterpiece Theater together on the telly. When my wife is out of town, a void is created and I have to find a substitute for human contact. What can I do differently? I usually eat Subway sandwiches for lunch and rather than buying a batch of sandwiches and eating them at home, I eat the sandwiches at the Subway. This gives me the opportunity to chitchat with my friends who work at Subway. I can either write at home or at my local Barnes & Noble. I pack up my laptop, go to Barnes & Noble and get to chat with the many friendly and knowledgeable employees. This is also the time I catch up with old friends via coffee, lunch or dinner engagements.

I work out daily at the local gym. I have made a conscious effort to create a small support network at the gym that keeps me motivated to show up every day. It also provides a new circle of friends. I have also located a writers support group that meets monthly. I used to play a lot of backgammon and have maintained my link with my backgammon friends who play every Thursday night. I always attend my men's Saturday support group when Kathy's out of town. My preference is to hang out with my wife, but I also want to be supportive of Kathy's lifestyle and never want her to curtail her activities merely to please me.

I am a terrible listener; I love to talk (some would say preach). This can be advantageous when lecturing or perhaps counseling. In personal relationships you run the risk of creating a counselor/client relationship that doesn't allow the friendship to flourish in an uninhibited way that allows love, warmth and understanding to flow easily. What can I do differently? I have to remember to be a friend rather than a counselor. I also have to remember that Kathy is my wife and not a counseling client; this requires a partnership relationship that focuses on love and trust vs. the identification of problems and strategies to correct. I'm sure some of my friends would empathize with Ann Quindlen's husband who once said to his wife (who is a published writer and a former columnist for the New York Times), "Do you think you could get me a beer and not write a column about it?" Similar problem, she has to remember to shed her role as a writer and assume her role as a wife and partner.

We always have choices. When we allow ourselves to examine all the options and are willing to risk and learn new behavior, desirable solutions can be found.

Relationships

**What do we live for, if not to make
life less difficult for each other?**

George Eliot

Wouldn't it be great to find the right person that fulfills all your needs and live happily ever after? One stop shopping is a myth; no one person can fulfill all your needs. This is one of the damaging myths we grow up with and bring into marriages. This unrealistic expectation puts a tremendous burden on relationships. Not only can the other not fulfill all your needs; the other person (if healthy) doesn't believe they were put on this planet only to serve you. Your partner also has an agenda and interests that will never completely coincide with yours.

Another myth is that, once you find your soul mate, you are going to **easily** live happily ever after. I am suspicious of any relationship that has never encountered rough passages. I think that you learn with experience how to navigate these troubled waters. And how can you learn to do that unless have encountered difficulties? All healthy relationships require negotiation to bridge the differences. It's not the differences that do the damage; it's the lack of willingness or skills to negotiate. Now if the differences are too great and the paths you are on are too divergent, the reason you got together in the first place is suspect and you have to accept the possibility that maybe you both need to go your own ways. If, for instance, one wants kids and the other doesn't, the gap might be too great to bridge.

When we begin to accept that we are totally responsible for our happiness and happiness comes from within, we lower the level of expectation and this lessens the possibility that the other will disappoint. When we let go of these myths about relationships, we then have the opportunity to create a real and meaningful one.

I am happily married to a person that is incredibly different from me. John Grey's book *Men Are From Mars; Women are from Venus* doesn't adequately describe the differences. We feel that we are from different galaxies. We went to four different marriage counselors looking for ways to make it work. The last counselor's comments felt like last rites were being performed on our relationship. He couldn't fathom how we got together and why we were together. Kathy and I knew that if we could make it work, we would have a great marriage. My marriage to Kathy is now at the top of my gratitude list. We love each other and have learned to accept the differences. We agree to disagree often and we have gotten much better at negotiating the differences. I have learned not to ask Kathy for that which she doesn't possess. It doesn't make Kathy a bad person; how can she give what she doesn't possess? It's like shopping for an ice cream cone in a hardware store. You are in the wrong store.

One summer I was thinking about doing some rollerblading for exercise and shared this with Kathy. Her response was "You will break every bone in your body". Kathy cannot be supportive of anything that she perceives to be dangerous. I shouldn't expect support or enthusiasm for this type of activity from Kathy. There is 65 year old man with the build of an ex-professional athlete who rollerblades in the park where I take my daily walk. This is the individual

I should be talking to about rollerblading. We often assume that if someone loves us they should also be unconditionally supportive. I think connecting the two is unfair to the relationship and forces spouses to pretend to be what they are not. I don't have to go shopping all day and Kathy doesn't have to sit in a duck blind during hunting season.

We get hung up on the negative aspects of our relationships. Learn to focus on what's right rather than what's wrong with the relationship. No relationship is perfect and I think that it's in our best interest to avoid or sidestep the negative aspects of a relationship. I'm a big believer in being a positive thinker and attempt to avoid negativity and negative people at all costs. When Kathy is in a victim mode and wants to complain excessively about the unfairness of the world, I am not the person to lend a sympathetic ear. Kathy knows this and doesn't burden our relationship with it. I'm in empathy with the Buddhist monk who slapped one of his disciples upside the head after he had made some negative comment and said, "Don't walk in my mind with your dirty shoes on."

Contribution And Service

**When you are good to others,
you are best to yourself.**

Ben Franklin

If you won the lottery (40 million big ones), what would you do in your spare time? The answer will give you an inkling as to what your real passions are and point you in the direction that your life needs to go. People will often respond that they would give some of the money to those less fortunate or that they would be freed up to help others in some fashion. These people have good instincts and understand that service and contribution is the path that leads to real fulfillment.

We are motivated by different things based on a level of awareness as to where real joy resides. We begin being motivated by the accumulation of wealth and material things. We discover that this isn't the total answer. Many will then seek some form of excellence and attempt to be the best they can be (the best computer programmer, the best writer, achieve the highest level of physical fitness, pursue an advanced degree or achieve some other high honor) and discover that this isn't the total answer. After much work and accumulation of life experiences, many discover that contribution and service is the ultimate calling. Proof of this is provided by the many examples of highly successful people whose lives evolve from being totally focused on their career into a life in which service and contribution play a significant role. Well-grounded people who have participated in some form of service or contribution rarely abandon it totally to pursue the accumulation of excessive wealth. If we aren't there for each other, what is the point and purpose of existence?

Buckminster Fuller opined "There are no passengers on spaceship Earth, only crew," and "You do not belong to you. You belong to the universe. The significance of you will remain forever obscure to you, but you may assume you are fulfilling your significance if you apply yourself to converting all your experience to the highest advantage of others."

Albert Schweitzer said "I don't know what your destiny will be, but one thing I know: the only ones among you who will really be happy are those who have sought and found how to serve."

A life of service can be noble, uplifting and fulfilling; it can also cause burnout and disillusionment. When fantasy obscures reality, good intentions can degenerate into feelings of frustration. Don't expect others to give what they don't have. Some might not be able to say thank you or show any form of gratitude.

What's the criterion for how much and what you should give? Ask yourself, are you giving or contributing in a way that fills you with energy? If your contributions or method of service depletes you and resentment is felt, then your talents will be wasted. Your contributions will not genuinely serve others.

I have learned to be very selective about those I counsel. If people are unable to receive and understand my message, my energy is depleted. It's a waste of time for both parties. I've discovered that if I convince people with a strong sell that they need counseling, I obtain clients in which the necessary chemistry is lacking in our relationship and they aren't good candidates for change. The process produces only marginal results. I can't be an effective catalyst with those that don't see merit in what I say. I now limit my services to those who request counseling after attending one of my seminars. I now have a smaller counseling practice. It's a much more pleasurable component of my life. Counseling suitable clients energizes me and makes me more alive, creative and productive in the other areas of my life. Our gift and services are really only effective when both parties are empowered by the process.

Letting Go

> **Anything you want can be acquired through detachment, because detachment is based on the unquestioning belief in the power of your true self.**
>
> *Deepak Choprah*

When you detach from expectations, you free energy. Think of the energy wasted in bitter disappointments and regrets. Think of the time wasted when you brood about past failures (i.e., unfulfilled expectations). Think about the self-inflicted pain caused by asking all those "what if" questions about the past that burdens us with sadness. Whenever a thought or past remembrance creates emotional pain, you are still linked to the event.

We often misunderstand the purpose of forgiveness. Forgiveness is a form of detachment. It isn't necessarily to make the *other* person whole, it's to allow *you* to disengage, uncouple, let go and place your focus on more positive matters. Forgiveness frees up energy that can be put to a more positive use in living life.

The risk with being emotionally linked to expectations is that you do not have absolute control over external events; you put yourself at the mercy of that which you can't entirely control. When events go according to plan, you are happy. When outcomes present you with nasty surprises, you are devastated. It's OK to plan the action, but it's folly to plan and totally anticipate the result.

I think the formula that combines serenity with the feeling of fulfillment that comes from being productive is to work hard and expect little. This isn't justification for pessimism or an indictment of optimism; it's an argument for acceptance. Detachment provides a closer connection to reality in the form of acknowledging that you really can't effectively micromanage all events or perfectly predict the future.

I make many short-term investments in the stock market. I do my analysis, make the best decisions I can and then I have to let go of expectations. My energy and focus is then available for other activities such as writing and preparing seminars.

A friend of mine recently was named salesman of the year at his company's annual award banquet; later that week he was diagnosed with prostate cancer. We have to learn that no matter what we plan or how hard we try, we win some and we lose some. Acceptance of that which we can't control, anticipate or predict makes the journey through life a lot easier.

By detachment, I don't mean passive living in which you only sit and watch the world go by (although I enjoy that at times). It means the conservation of energy by not expending energy and emotions on trying to control the uncontrollable. The only things you have direct control over are yourself and your perceptions.

Highly successful people practice detachment; they are very efficient (conserve energy) and focus on possibilities, rather than worrying over past events or activities outside their sphere of influence. Successful managers deal in reality and ask, "What can we do now?" Detachment doesn't mean indifference or apathy; it means understanding reality and valuing life.